Living or Retiring

in Mexico

All you need to know
before you go

by Leo Buijs

*To all our Mexican and gringo friends
who made us feel at home,
away from home.*

First edition 2016, updated second edition 2018

National Library of Canada Cataloging in Publication

Buijs, Leo,
   Living/ Retiring in Mexico/ Mexico travel/ Leo Buijs

Includes index.
ISBN 978-0973552751

1. Living or Retiring in Mexico 2. Mexico Travel information 3. guidebook to living or retiring in Mexico 4. Baja California – Mexico – I Title

This book is published by Seaview Investments Ltd.,
219 Spindrift Rd, Courtenay B.C. V9N 9S9 Canada

E-mail: leobuijs@yahoo.ca

Cover design and layout: Desgraph.Ltd.

…. Could it be that Americans are a restless people, a mobile people, never satisfied with where they are as a matter of selection?

From travels with Charley, by John Steinbeck

Other books by

Leo Buijs

50 Best Dog Walks Around Victoria
2003
Best Dog Walks on Vancouver Island
2008
Beers of British Columbia
2010
Children around the World
2015 edition
Children around the World
large coffee-table edition
2016
A Taste of Living in Mexico
2016

Map of the United States of Mexico

Table of Contents

The Fun Part

Food and Drinks

The not so Fun Part

The Important stuff

Introduction

This book has a fair number of Spanish words and terminology. It should not turn you off, as I made sure there is an explanation right after the words and if not, you can find it in a glossary that I put for your reference in the back of the book.

To have certain subjects clustered together, it makes for a better overview of that chapter's subject. The book has five main chapters. This one being the introduction to the subjects and to staying in Mexico in general.

The following part is about the fun things to do and explore in Mexico, followed by a chapter of not so fun experiences. These are to make you aware of things that can happen in a foreign country like Mexico. Customs and rules are quite different from what we are used to.

The next chapter is more fun again as it is all about food and beverages in Mexico. Informative and entertaining, I hope, just like the other chapters.

Last but not least, is the chapter on important things to know before you go, like passports, car license, utilities and insurance. Maybe not so entertaining, but important enough to work yourself through it if you are serious about spending more time in Mexico.

So here we go

Millions of people vacation every year in Mexico. How many of them, while there, being lazy on a beach or next to a pool with a tasty margarita or cool beer in hand, are having visions of that life on a permanent basis? A second home, away from home or a complete change of lifestyle and settling permanently somewhere in Mexico.

Some people would trade their hurried lifestyle in a wink if they could. Others would be a bit more careful and check out what

options there are and how they can accomplish that dream.
This book is for both: fast movers and the more 'wait and see'
types. Both of you will find a lot of useful substance in this book
as it contains a wealth of information and first-hand experiences
I learned during 15 years of traveling, living and retiring in Mexico
with my wife and dog.

As a habit, I always have been taking travel notes, often at
nocturnal hours, wherever we went. We did it all: frequent
traveling throughout this beautiful and cultural diverse country,
rented long-term accommodations in different States and
eventually bought and built a house with ocean view and a five-
minute walk to an unspoiled beach. Those things are possible in
Mexico and you don't have to be very rich to accomplish that.
It has been a long and steady up-hill learning curve for us and
you can take advantage of it by harvesting the results. We have
experienced the ups and downs about living and owning real-
estate in Mexico and as they say; "I can write a book about it."

And so, I did.

This book however, is very different from all the other books
available on this subject. During one of our extended stays in
2001, I picked up a writing job as a freelance journalist for a bi-
weekly English language newspaper in Mexico.

As it happened, my earliest experience was a local event I wrote
about, submitted to the local English language newspaper and
had it published instantly. Twelve years later I was still writing for
that same paper with a deadline every other week, which was a
great thing for an early retired guy like me. To have a dead-line
every other week surely kept me on my toes and out of trouble.
For over a decade I have been writing on subjects like fiestas,
cultural events, Mexican bureaucracy, and what to do and not to

do in Mexico. Some of the best articles of that time are used or updated and therefore you will get a real taste of living in Mexico in the following chapters.

-0-0-0-0-

What attracts foreigners to live in Mexico?

There are a million answers to this simple question. Perhaps John Steinbeck touched a chord when he wrote in *Travels with Charley*, "Could it be that Americans and Canadians are a restless people, a mobile people, never satisfied with where they are as a matter of selection?"

Much has been written about North Americans retiring to Mexico to live out their Golden Years. However, during the last few years I have seen an increasing number of younger people moving to Mexico. They did not come to retire necessarily as yet. They came alone or with young families to combine work with fun. Some of them further their careers with the companies that employ them (if they were lucky enough). Others are finding existing needs and starting their own businesses to fill certain needs, a niche in the market place, which they recognized.

When I asked people why they came to Mexico, the answers fell into three main categories; the weather, to be out of the rat-race and the different culture.

In those last five years, I have seen an increasing number of younger people moving to Mexico, not necessarily to retire but to further their career alongside a different life style. They often work long-distance with the help of internet and having the time of their life.

These folks are called the new Expats.

Many people have the false impression that you find a simpler life-style in Mexico. And that is true to a certain extent and the weather has a lot to do with this. But everyday life can turn out to be a nuisance at times.

Think about water: if you are lucky it runs from your tap every morning, is most of the time not potable, at times lacking pressure or at odd times not even available. So, you need to be flexible and sparse with water. Better still is to have a certain capacity of reserve water for your shower or laundry. For drinking and washing your vegetables and berries, you bring in the large heavy 19-liter blue bottles. Living off grid poses other problems such as battery maintenance and cleaning of your sun panels on regular intervals. Safety and a language barrier present other issues that come to mind, but they offer also a challenge. Learning a new language can be exciting and fulfilling by itself.

Perhaps other things make up for the inconvenience, like living closer to nature, maybe within view of an unspoiled beach. As land is relatively cheap, you might have a larger property than you would have had north of the border. With that you might get the problem of hiring a gardener. Of course, all those things can be managed by a property management company, but that comes usually with a North American price tag.

Choosing to live in a town or a larger, perhaps historical city, water and electricity are less of a problem and or completely out of your control.

Still, a lot of us would take some inconveniences to get out of the rat-race, leaving that stressful life behind and acquire a new lifestyle. To live in a different, warm and sunny country where you can be anybody you would like to be without pretense. This, among other things, has a perpetual pull to *'la Vida Loca'* in Mexico. Not everybody is cut out for this and that's why not everyone's dream comes through. It takes a certain personality to make that big step. Many of our friends and acquaintances in

Mexico are 'different' to say the least. Individualistic characters are the most common denominator.

Creative individuals, often with artistic aspirations live next to renegades, non-conformists, freaks and oddballs or occasionally, plain nuts. But the beauty of it is that in this climate and culture one gets away with most of his or her idiosyncrasies.

There is a saying by boaters about ownership. It says: his best days were the day he got his boat and the other day was when he sold it. Well, this could also be said about owning a house in Mexico, but I must admit that the time in between has been very exciting and educational and that is what this book is all about.

This book is a compilation of Mexican adventures, experiences, food and fiestas, put together and easy to read as each part contains smaller chapters revealing life in Mexico.

My story is based upon observations and firsthand experiences during some decades traveling to and living half of that time in Mexico. I make no pretense to thoroughness, but have tried. It is the same for objectivity, which was not easy.

All information including tips on location and geographical differences, climate, prices, tax and government related info such as customs immigration etcetera are believed accurate at the time of writing. As things can change rather quickly in Mexico, I cannot be held liable for changes, omissions or mistakes. Thank you for getting this book and enjoy the ride!

If not for this book, where to start?

To get a real taste of Mexico, my advice is to take some trips to different parts of Mexico as the country is quite large and very different from one part to the other. Perhaps you have done that already and found out that not everyone likes to spend all their time on the beach or besides a pool. Central Mexico with its mountains and historic towns have a totally different climate compared to the coastal areas and a different culture, and an even warmer climate can be found further south.

My wife and I have been traveling to Mexico many times for shorter trips, and then one year, we were in a position to explore this sunny and colorful country for months at the time. That was important for us to get a feel for it, to experience different areas and make a list of what our priorities were.

It turned out that for us, our stay should be drive-able. That does limit you if you don't want to spend half your time getting there and back. But the plus was to have a car and be able to bring lots of stuff including our inseparable house-pet: the dog. Not that you cannot fly with your dog, but it is limited. For instance, when temperatures heat up in April or May, airlines don't take dogs any more. Over the Christmas holidays, our carrier from Canada does not allow dogs in cargo. O.K., if you have a small *chihuahua*, you might put the little one under the seat, but larger size dogs have more restrictions and travel in cargo.

So, connectivity either by road or plane can be an important factor for choosing your Mexican stay.

I have been going to Mexico since 1984. First on the east side, the State of Yucatan with all its historic Mayan ruins, lovely beaches and superb diving spots around the island of Cozumel. I have been back there a few more times and it took until the late nineties that I finally decided to check out the Pacific side and Central Mexico with it's beautiful colonial cities. On the Pacific side, we drove the entire Baja California peninsula, north and south, more than ten times. However, the first time we flew as part of a booked all-inclusive hotel package in San Jose del Cabo and extended our stay for a week or two to explore the rest of the southern peninsula. We rented a car and drove counter clockwise to check out the famous reef at Cabo Pulmo in the Sea of Cortez. We went on to the humble, at that time, little capital of the State, La Paz. It was very small and sleepy still, at that time, except for weekends on the Malecón After checking the beaches north from there, we went south-west to the sleepy town of Todos Santos.

Finding a hotel for a few nights was difficult. The now famous Hotel California was in disrepair, closed-up and for sale. We inquired about the price and what the options were, but never got an appointment to see the place inside. The few accommodations there were, were either cockroach infested, very cheap places or high-end luxury rooms in small historic haciendas.

There was virtually nothing in between, making the future of Hotel California a plausible success. We surely fell in love with the town. One morning at the beach, we had seen already several whales passing by, but then suddenly we saw a presumably, mother whale with a small calf playing, frolicking, not further out than perhaps 100 yards from the beach. Mommy showing the baby how to jump and roll in the waves. It was a breathtaking experience! Watching this from an unspoiled, virgin beach made this so much better and different from the tourist-trodden beaches of so many Mexican destinations. This was unbelievable! Baja California has miles of unspoiled beaches with whales passing by, up close from December to March.

Good things usually end to quickly, so we went on reluctantly to the spoiled tourist town of Cabo San Lucas to finish our circle and went home the next day. It took us a few years to come back but not until after we checked out the Mexican mainland: Mexico City, Quaretaro, Guanajuato and San Miguel. Beautiful cities each in their own way. Historic pearls in a large quilt of places high in the mountains with colder temperatures in winter and no beaches. That made us decide to go back to Baja California in 2001. This was the first time we drove the entire length of the peninsula from the Tijuana border to San Jose at the Sea of Cortez. We had rented an apartment for a month in San Jose del Cabo and brought our bicycles to explore the area other than just by car. Our home-stay was close to the golf course and municipal tennis courts, so we played most mornings right at seven o'clock because later in the day it was quite hot that November.

A year later we rented a *casita* in Loreto, halfway down the Baja right on the Sea of Cortez. This was a spectacular setting, as every morning we had the sun come up out of the sea and burn through the thin curtains from where we saw the calm morning waters of the Sea of Cortez with some islands speckled in the distance. By 10.30 it would become a different matter. The winds would pick up and transform the so quiet Sea of Cortez into a white capped fury by lunch time. The town has a nice older centre and historic mission. We explored the mountains and the shores far south and north from there. Our trip to the mission of San Javier, built in 1697, still standing and very isolated in the mountains at that time, was quite the adventure. Particularly the road up to it, as we had to cross river beds and steep mountain roads more like goat paths and only doable with a 4x4. Now that road is all black topped as far as I know. One must go further into the mountains to find adventure.

After a month and a half, we moved down to Todos Santos where we had booked a *casita* on the huge palm-covered grounds of artist Nanette Hayles. This was close to the center of town and was the first year the Todos Santos Film Fest was organized.

Everything was very informal, small scaled and personal. Also, it was cold and rainy, and the Theatre de Leon was a massive draft hole with concrete seats that numbed your butt in no time. Smart people brought pillows and blankets to make it through the often-lengthy Mexican dramatic movies.

This trip in 2004 ultimately resulted in us buying a house in Mexico.

-0-0-0-0-

Where to go in Mexico?

Depending on where you live north of the border, central, east or west and if you would like to drive the distance or rather fly, your options are endless. Generally, mainland Mexico offers more affordable accommodation as compared to the sunny southern Baja California. We checked out both. While staying for a month in the historic town of San Miguel, we did day-trips to the larger surrounding central Mexico cities. We loved Guanajuato with it's underground road network and relative quiet pedestrian friendly old center. As a university city, it has a good energizing vibe to it with a varied and busy cultural agenda.

Following is an excerpt from my notes how we got to SMA, as San Miguel de Allende is called by insiders. The year is 1999 and we flew into Mexico City where we took a fast and comfortable Intercity bus to Querétaro, from where we had to take a smaller local bus.

Sitting nearly at the back of an old second-class bus, I watched the sky through the side-window changing from purple-orange to pitch-black. Around me people were standing and some hanging over me with their awkward carried-on bundles of who knows what. The bus was rushing along a perilous winding mountain road. And on the other side of the bus was a lightning- storm approaching, making snapshots of us every so often and lightning up the spooky countryside.

It felt so surreal, sitting on that small, hard-seat, bouncing along and not even knowing where to get off. At the opposite side, in the distance over the mountains, there was still a wonderful glowing red sky but my view was very limited by the standing peasants next to me.

After a few stops, there was a little bit standing room coming free that I took up to make sure I could get off when needed. I knew I had to get off somewhere after about an hour's ride through the Mexican country side but was not sure when exactly. Nobody that I tried to communicate with spoke any English and my Spanish was as good as their English. Looking at my watch I noticed the hour on the bus had passed and now I was getting really nervous as complete darkness had set in.

Then suddenly, far below, the town of San Miguel with its many illuminated church spires unmistakably announced itself. The bus's brakes squeaked all the way down the steep road into the town in the valley below which extends along the mountainside, When I finally got off, I had to remind the driver to open the large compartments below, where I had to seek through lots of other parcels to find my own luggage.

Over hugely uneven cobblestones, I dragged my suitcase into the bus-station to get to the front where two taxis were waiting anxiously for business. The first one had an open loading platform at the back and it was just as easy to throw everything in there as opposed to try fitting it in a small trunk of the other taxi. And as the rain had abated, that's the one we took.

"Address?" the driver asked when I tried to fit my legs in the small space he had up front. I came prepared and showed him a piece of paper with the street name in case I would pronounce it wrong and yes, it came in handy. It didn't provoke any direct response, so I asked how much it would be, knowing that they have a set rate in San Miguel. Being slightly higher at night, he told me it was Vente pesos, or the equivalent of two dollars US. Welcome to the expatriate lifestyle.

With the nice temperature, the windows were down, and the strangest scents whiffed through the car but none that called up any recognizable memories despite the fact I had been to Mexico at least half a dozen times. 'This is different' I noticed, different from Cancun in Yucatan, Puerto Vallarta at the other side or Baja California. 'A whole new adventure.'

San Miguel de Allende is in the central highlands and most afternoons has a rainstorm in November and can be quite cool at night. The historic town is one of the more popular overwintering places for gringos. There is quite a large expat community with lots of programs especially designed for the English-speaking community. A decent English library and weekly newsletter is very helpful in keeping in touch with same-minded snow-birders or expats.

Easter is very special anywhere in Mexico, but the Saturday before is quite a mind-blowing experience in SMA, as fire cracker figurines impersonating Judas are blown up from the plaza in front of the beautiful cathedral. Slaughtering is not such a shocking event in Mexico because kids are eagerly looking for an arm or a leg around the plaza.

Everything in Mexico is symbolic or has a meaning or a cause. Churches have mostly only one steeple as a second tower used to cost more taxes to motherland Spain during colonial times.

The Institute de Allende in San Miguel has superb art classes and a very good Spanish language program. The morning I checked it out an old custodian was opening the Allende museum and looked up at the clock on the steeple for the time as he had no watch. Our gardeners never had watches either, they always had to ask the time. Perhaps that was why they were mostly late on the job. What becomes apparent is, you must adjust to Mexican time. It took us always a week or two, to really slow down and appreciate the word *'manjana.'* As that is a very common expression anywhere in Mexico. *Manjana, manjana,* can be any time, as opposed to *ahora,* meaning now, but that can still mean within the hour or sometime today.

We lived right in the center of the old town, very close the convent where we often went for an espresso and apple strudel while facing the magnificent murals by Alfaro Siqueiros. It sure was a wonderful time.

A few last comments on SMA. San Miguel is not like your average over-wintering paradise. It has a golf-course outside the town which is not bad. But the town's appeal comes mainly from its rich cultural events, historical heritage and a core of English speaking expatriates. This has attracted many art-schools and good quality language institutes. With that, there has flourished a profuse number of art-galleries and upscale restaurants. With the real-estate boom, the number of interior decorators has sky-rocketed and mixed in between, you find a large number of gift-shops, coffee-shops and Internet cafes.

Another popular area for settlement is around Lake Chapala, further south-west of the central mountains. A very pleasant climate called 'Eternal Spring' combines with picturesque towns along the north shore of the lake. The area has good access by air to the large, culture-rich city of Guadalajara which is about an hour north.

Snowbirds used to have lots in common, but that is changing. However, they still travel south around the same time and always are in search for agreeable weather conditions, have similar hobbies, such as golf, tennis or surfing.

We have been a few times to Puerto Vallarta. The area north west from town is very popular by expats and it is a good location in terms of direct international flights. The old town is nice but very touristy and the best beaches are north and south from here. Lots of 'snow-birders' live here next to permanent ex-pats. In February and March this exotic destination becomes more crowded with weekly north American vacationers browsing the area once they get out of the all-inclusive hotels.

Cruise-ship passengers also make the old town busy on certain days and this also counts for places like Cabo, Cancun and Huixtla further south. We liked the fact that we could charter a boat from the Nuevo Marina. The Bay of Banderas offers great sailing with easy day-trip destinations to the off-shore island at the edge of the Pacific. Some good snorkel and deep-sea diving spots are accessible faster by speedboat. The weather is most of the time very nice but can be humid at times and while we were there, we lived through a serious 7.4 earthquake.

At the opposite side of the country there is the easy accessible area around Cancun. This part of the State of Yucatan area offers huge choices in apartment complexes in Playa del Carmen and other protected neighborhoods.
The old town of Merida has become very popular and the history of the 'sites' in Yucatan such as Chitzen Itza, Uxmal and Tulum have a permanent appeal to vacationers and snowbirds alike.

The islands Cozumel and Isla Mueres have their own charm and are of particular interest to divers and beach combers. The weather is always nice except for the hurricane season that can begin in May and extends to October and is hot and humid. The Atlantic side usually has more storms then the Pacific side, but now with extreme weather changes, there is no way to predict how that will work out in the future.

-0-0-0-0-

First trips to Baja California by car.

Our departure was on an unusually cold day for Victoria BC, in January. The day before, we had to make the decision to leave the kayak that we had hoped to bring, at home as it was under a layer of fresh blown snow and could not be moved without damaging it. A few last things were carefully packed in an ice and snow-covered Volvo station wagon. With weather like that, it felt quite good to leave the slippery and windblown driveway in -8 Celsius.

Lining up for the Coho ferry to Port Angeles, Washington, an older US customs officer checked everybody's car under the hood. I had no idea how to open ours. While I am trying to locate the release handle, he asked where we are going and for how long.

"Loreto, Baja California" I say.

"That place from Butterfield?" he asked.

"No," I say, "we rented a casita for the month on the waterfront."

"How much is that," he asked again, "and how much for a two bedroom?"

Strange questions for a customs officer and when he saw our dog in the back, he lost all interest in us and our papers.

A second custom inspection when we drove off the ferry didn't take long but then we got a shock. This Sunday, the last of the Holiday season, the roads were busy and covered with ice and drifting snow as nothing was cleared or salted. So, the actual start on our 4,000-km trip became a crawl over Highway 101, which had no separator in the middle at the time and was sometimes three lanes, making it a dangerous road.

The way we like to travel is going against the rush-hour flows. So we reach Sacramento by the end of the day while the outbound lanes are busy and inbound relatively quiet. The advantage of sleeping near the old town is avoiding rush hour the next morning. So, early the next morning we just drive out of town, the opposite of most traffic. This way getting out of Sacramento is a breeze. Just get into the left lane and put the peddle to the metal. Traffic is usually not bad on the I5 and only at about an hour and a half before reaching LA, it gets really busy. If you can plan this, try reaching down town over lunch-time. This has worked for us beautifully many a times.

The girl at the desk at our motel in Carlsbad told us that rush-hour into San Diego would be over after 10am. Well, we didn't have the patience, so by 9 am we were on the I5 again and got into some heavy traffic that slowed down to crawl speed at times. Still we made the Mexican border in about an hour and were filling out entry forms at customs and immigration. The visa was $ 20 this time per person. Nobody looked at anything. Nowadays, you have to press a button and if you hit green you're in Tijuana, Mexico. With red, they pull you over for an inspection which normally doesn't take long.

As the road connections change from year to year, we missed an important turn off in Tijuana. This should be avoided at all cost. It is not something you wish to even your worst enemy. Driving around Tijuana, not knowing where you are going can turn into a nightmare. It took us the better part of an hour to find our way to a sign called 'scenic highway'. The toll-road that is, 24 pesos at the time, with three check-points before reaching Ensenada where the road skims around the beautiful bay.

The contrast, from the mega-hub of San Diego with 12 lane freeway clogged with the nicest luxury cars and many trucks, huge grocery stores, nice looking restaurants and shopping malls from here to eternity and then suddenly this; two-lane highway without hardly any traffic, mostly old cars, no Malls or large food stores any more, just mini outlets and vegetable stalls here and there, corrugated sheet-metal shacks instead of properly lined up sub-divisions.

What a pleasure to leave the multi lanes around San Diego behind and drive the quiet two-lane toll-road. To be king of the road again on winding blacktop along beaches with surf and among rocky outcrops, such a treat!

By Ensenada, there is some congestion for about 25 km south of town. Once past the first Military stop*, the road climbs up into the mountains and nobody is in your way again for hours. This is relaxed driving despite the narrow road and many 'Curva peligrosas'. It feels instantly vacation, was it not for the dirt along the road. The plastic garbage is a shining, constant reflecting menace and pure shame that's particularly noticeable in this northern section of the Baja. Strips of about 40 to 50 feet wide, along both sides of the road, are completely covered in non-decomposing plastic bags, bottles, tires and junk!

* Along the nearly 1000-mile highway to Cabo San Lucas are about 5 military stops that inspect your car for fire-arms and drugs. It's not a big deal most of the time, but going north, it can cause some delays.

A day later... by 9.30 we were in El Rosario where it is advisable to fill up for fuel. This is the last Pemex gas-station before the large National Park with the fantastic cacti and obelisk size boulder formations. This is a beautiful part of the trip and if you have the time, staying overnight at the hotel in Catavina is a rewarding experience.

From here it is a few hours to the next town of any size, Guerrero Negro which is just past the state border of Baja California Sur. You get the bottom of your car sprayed (10 pesos, which is for agricultural protection). It is also on the border of a time-zone.

Moving from Pacific to Mountain time, losing an hour. This is a great place if you want to get close to the whales. Lots of whale-watching tour offerings from December to March.

Day 7 *(yes, we took our time)*
During my dog-walk, it was warming up quickly from a very cold night in San Ignacio, a small but amazing oasis town with an old Mission right in the center of the village. Now we had an exciting day ahead as we drove towards the east coast of the peninsula, to the magnificent Sea of Cortez made famous by explorers and writers (Jacques Cousteau and John Steinbeck). Exactly as two years ago, we came into the French Colonial town of Santa Rosalia on a Saturday morning. Just like then, we used the only ATM machine in town and picked up fresh bread and sweets at the famous El Boleo Bakery. We stocked up on fuel and vegetables, so we could camp out for the night as was the plan. We went on to Mulegé where the nicest part of the trip begins along the beaches of the Bay of Conception.

The next town of importance, Loreto.
This town was the first Mission in upper and lower California.

You would expect someone that arrives for the third time in this historic little gem in Baja California Sur, to drive straight into town, particularly if he did it right the first two times. We were probably too eager and for that matter took an exit too early off the Trans-Peninsular Highway.
It was immediately noticeable that the town, despite being a Sunday, was busier than ever before. While checking in at our bungalow we heard a plane take off and that was not the last one for the day. Before, there used to fly only two or three planes in and out during the week.
Again, this time, the town had been trashed by a hurricane, late

in October while in 2001 the town was hit in September quite badly. Most businesses are still the same. Like Café Ole, where the retired male gringos congregate each morning. It still offers lousy coffee. Dos Equis Amber is still hard to find or maybe impossible to buy here as it starts to look now after going through many different stores and beer outlets. The supermarket 'El Pescadores' is busier but still has a poor selection and no vegetables to speak off. Prices have not changed much either or does it just feel that way now our Canadian loonie has substantial more buying power than before?

During previous visits the town was very quiet, but now on Sunday evening, the Malecón was one big macho spectacle. Young muscular Mexican guys with shiny cars and pickups running on oversized tires, loud mufflers or hugely amplified boom boxes, were trying to impress the sexy girls in town. Apparently, this phenomenon repeats itself three times a week, and with having our rented bungalow right on the Malecón, earplugs became an absolute necessity from Friday- to Sunday night.

A month later, after we arrived in Todos Santos, we were soon to be found house-hunting. Why?

We came to realize that renting a casita for months and staying in hotel rooms are not the best way to experience Mexico. Because of our dog we often could not find decent accommodation. People without pets won't run into this problem of course, but once you have a pet, most rental places and hotels in Mexico avoid you like the plague.

The question became 'How do we get out of this uncomfortable situation?'

At night, as it cooled down quickly because this is desert area, we were often inside, sitting on a folding chair because we found the couch uncomfortable or dirty. The casita had a concrete slab floor with geckos all around us. They come out particularly at night. Cockroaches were not uncommon, mice and ants; do I have to say more?

We were wondering why we always ended up in cold and uncomfortable places? There was no alternative as long as we would travel with the dog. We did spend way more on accommodation this time than ever before and still are ending up in dumps.

Was it all an 'idea fixe', we wondered, renting property and being away for months at the time?

This led to the realization that we could do better.

When we drove north from Todos Santos to La Pastoras, the surf-beach about two miles out of town, we had seen a nice traditional Mexican home on a half-acre overlooking the ocean and only a five-minute walk to a glorious beach. We fell in love instantly with this house. But we never do things impulsively, so we checked some other places for comparison. This is how we met Paola, chef cook at the culinary Santa Fee Restaurant, as he had his house for sale privately. His house had a nice inner courtyard with a lovely garden that had a large variety of salads, legumes and herbs growing. Planted in November he said, now early February, ready to harvest. Ten feet from his kitchen, the garlic smell was so strong that I had trouble getting into his superbly equipped kitchen.

The house was not it for us and lacked ocean view. We checked a few more places and went back to our dream-home to make the walk to the beach from there. Already on the way down we saw the whale sprays. So many, so frequent and so close to shore. What a magical place! In the surf at La Pastoras, which was not even great today, were 8 or 10 surfers. But at a short distance behind them were at least a dozen whales, some with babies. What a spectacle to watch. Needless to say, that we started to feel better and better about this place. We realized that not everything is perfect, that is life! A few things have to change or added before we would move in. But the overall feeling, the gut-feeling was good about it. This time, our third time in Todos Santos, our dollar was much stronger, and we might be in a position to fulfill a long-time dream. We didn't know that the urge for home-ownership was still there, but as soon as we arrived in Todos Santos and you see the magic from all that sudden lushness after driving through desert for a few days, you get the feeling; this is the place to be.

Las Tunas, just one mile out of Todos Santos, seems to be the better neighborhood. Real estate agents live there, editors from New York fashion magazines live there while working by satellite connection. The personal friend and manager from Joan Baez was living two homes down. It's the latest development about 10 minutes from town because of the poor condition of the road. It's under two kilometers, but very bumpy, no electricity and no phone lines. A cell-phone is a must here. The house has a generator and a solar system, and the most important thing, plenty of water. There is city water and the magical canal system that fills on demand with Ejido spring water. We looked around here four years ago, the land and everything else was so desert, dry and bare. Now after the aqua-culture system has been in place, mature gardens grow in a matter of a few years.

Still doubts

We felt that this house we found, might fill the gap and get us out the uncomfortable rental situation, but still there were doubts as you can read in the following paragraph.

Do we still want to live in Mexico, four or six months a year? We are now about six weeks away from home and I feel losing control of the affairs at home. I have no idea what is in our bank account and if we are being paid for things we should be.
The internet café here apparently has no secure provider that allows me to get into my on-line banking. (remember, this is 2003)
How would 5 or 6 months' work out? We seem not to miss the kids. As long as we can call them and hear good things, and how much fun they have together, they don't need us anymore. We are 'empty nesters,' aren't we? Retired and can go anywhere we like. (Have checked out Hawaii, Costa Rica a few times, the latter is too far to drive, and Hawaii has a strict quarantine rule on dogs.) Later in the week we had friends over and spend two days with them around town. After a humongous breakfast at Café Todos Santos and visiting most of the galleries in town (Todos Santos is the only place I know where there are more galleries then taco stands) we went to the house we had a conditional offer on by now. Nice to get a second opinion, in this case from friends with similar tastes and interests. It was quite clear from the start that we were obviously not the only ones falling in love with the place. They liked the traditional tile work and couldn't get over the beauty and work that has gone into the garden. The water system was demonstrated by the vendor. Once she opened it up, the little canal was overflowing in about 5-10 minutes. She really proved the magical, nearly unlimited water supply in a place that is practically desert everywhere else in Baja.

Friday February 13th.

The day of the accepted offer. I will never forget the moment sitting around the dining table at the house we were buying, discussing the conditions, and suddenly I watched a whale breaching right in the distance. I was sold already on the place, but this gave me a very good feeling about it and I took it as a good omen. After some pulling back and forth we came to an agreement that made both parties happy. It was only until I had to sign, I realized it was Friday the 13th. We had no qualms about the date and surely believed, the deal won't have any detrimental effect on our dream.

To relieve the buildup stress from the morning's negotiations, we went for another beach walk right below our house. On the steep slanted beach there were two other people walking and what was good to see, picking the odd piece of garbage that lay at the high-water line. I was inclined to do the same before but felt a bit inhibited about it. Now I saw Keith who happens to be our new neighbour from Wisconsin, do it. I felt not so ridicules about it. It's now our beach and people better take care of it to keep it as virgin as it has been until now.

We made lists for things to bring that we had at home and other items that had to be acquired. We were of course very excited and had to see the notary a few times who would finish things off while we are back up north.

Tonight, at the Canada Del Diablo Bar, Joan Baez is doing a gig. To get in the open-air bar, we had to wait a long time. First some people had to leave before they could allow more people in and for a 60-peso cover charge, we made it just in time for Joan's performance. 'Christmas in Washington' was one of her first songs, followed by 'The Prisoner' which was well-received by the mixed but mostly elderly gringo crowd. 'Saving Grace,' and a few Latino/ Spanish songs went over even better, particularly with the locals. Drink tickets were sold in batches of 10 for 100 pesos. Three for a glass of wine or rum/coke and two for a beer. Joan had of course a few jokes to share and it proved she hasn't changed much. The President got a lot of crap in her version of the outcome of three calamities fixed up by the best surgeons in the States. Key words, horse's ass and cowboy hat. She was in town after a long tour in the U.K. and staying with a friend and business manager two houses down to the beach from our new place. We met them all, including Joan, Jeanie, her friend with look-a-like haircut and husband Rock. We met more interesting characters and they are all so nice! Every time they introduced us to someone else who welcomes us to the neighborhood.

And so, in 2004 we became owners after about 3 months of legalities to be worked out by the vendor and the notary we hired for closing the deal. As all property on the Baja peninsula falls in the restricted zone (see next chapter), most of the work was to prepare the so called *Fideicomiso*.

Currently a proposal to abolish this *'Fideicomiso'* system is at the Mexican senate level for the second time. First time it failed. Maybe this time too, but eventually abolishment is expected to follow through as it is predicted to boost property values and sales by 30% in a very short time.

-0-0-0-0-

How friendly are Mexicans?

The other day I came across this blog from Chuck Poulsen that describes exactly the way Mexican are. I have had many instances of the same friendly behavior by Mexican strangers.

"There is a very large and upscale mall in Guadalajara called the Galerias. One of the anchors is Liverpool, a Mexican retailer that the shopping crowd equates to Saks Fifth Avenue. The other anchor is Sears, which in Mexico sells much higher quality (and priced) merchandise than Sears in Canada or the U.S., strangely enough.

The only thing that had me in an upscale mall was a search for a jacket and a couple of ball caps. Mexicans don't wear caps like up north; they're hard to find. I saw a teenager in a store wearing a cap, backwards, of course, and asked him where he got it. His mother was with the kid and told him to walk with me to the store and show me where the caps were at.

All this fuzzy, feel good news from an unexpected source, namely me, is because Mexicans get a bum rap from Canadians and Americans.

I've been to Mexico many times and lived here for a couple of years awhile back.

Mexicans who live outside the tourist destinations are generally friendly, almost always helpful people with a very good sense of humor.

Of course, there are exceptions, but I dare say they are friendlier than your average Canadian or American.

-0-0-0-0-

Todos Santos Early Days

Todos Santos Early Days

During our second week stay we saw whales every day. Particularly off the beach by Todos Santos, where we had the best show of breaching Gray whales. A mother and calf were swimming side by side as if giving swimming lessons. Then they were jumping and tail smashing, excitement galore.

We loved the little town of Todos Santos, so green and authentic with a lot of tasteful galleries and a few historic buildings. The saying about Todos Santos is that it's the only place in Mexico where there are more art galleries than taco stands. Now don't get me wrong, but if you are looking for a tasty bite on the street, there are plenty of taco stands. Art galleries however, are numerous and of great quality.

We stayed a few extra days and had a good cappuccino with breakfast, local beers with lunch and Baja wine with dinner. That wine brought back memories from a trip to Kenya where we also paid a fortune for not such very good local wine. The alternative, import was out of reach! So what do you drink? (This has changed marvelously, the quality of the wine that is. However, the price is still high or equivalent to the price of wine north of the border.)

It was easy to fall in love with Southern Baja and Todos Santos in specific because of the weather and the endless options for water-sports. Surfing and beach combing nearby while snorkeling, diving, kayaking and sailing are possible almost everywhere else. Whale watching, same thing, absolutely tops! The moderate temperature and the fact that it has over 300 days of sunshine per year are hard to beat.

-0-0-0-0-

The Fun Part

To get in the mood

Imagine yourself on a patio with a margarita or Corona (fine, but not the best Mexican beer) and a plate full of quesadillas, Tabasco and guacamole on the side, a colourful tablecloth, the blue and white plastic table and chairs (provided by Corona) and an umbrella of course as it is sunny and warm. All Mexican icons in their own right and unmistakably part of the ex-pat's life in Mexico.

But there is so much more that makes Mexico, Mexico. Therefor I like to describe some typical Mexican styles that make homes and decorative items so special and appealing to us foreigners.

First the multi-hued, may I say wild colour combinations are something that stands out almost everywhere in Mexico. From house colours to traditional clothing and interior decor items. Graceful arched verandas are combined with warm ochre coloured walls and checker-board tile floors.

Modern homes now also experiment with sort of the opposite; a Minimalist style, simple and earthy colours opposed to the wild colour schemes.

Classy homes often make use of a Boveda, meaning- vaulted, rounded ceiling.

For wall decoration one can find very interesting stenciled or painted wall bands.

Interesting textiles are often naturally dyed woolen blankets and sarapas that are handwoven and come in vibrant colours that differ from state to state. Some places however, seldom dye wool and leave shawls or bedspreads in their natural colour. A texture of white on white brocade makes for subtle table linen.

Strangler-root palm or strangled beams are used decoratively indoors and out and are not cheap as they must come from central Mexico.

Another wood, used mostly indoors as a ceiling beam, are hand-hewn bacote. They are hand shaped hardwood beams that give lots of character to a house. An item that will give a nice touch to the interior are gauze-white curtains, while for the bedrooms sheer white mosquito netting might come in handy and will look very romantic.

A popular indoor-outdoor furniture is called Equipal. This has a rather rough wooden frame with leather seating and backs. The inside can also be upholstered with the colourful fabrics that look so typical Mexican.

The extreme colourful and craftily painted furniture comes from a town in the State of Michoacan. The large black pots are made in Chihuahua.

Ceramic animals come from Oaxaca and they also make the beautiful jars, and urns are called *Tala Vera*. Most tiles come from the town of Dolores Hidalgo, central Mexico. Cheaper tiles are called *Pueblo* tiles which are brown and earthy in tone. Tin mirrors and lamps are mostly made in San Miguel.

Beautifully decorated ceramic sinks are very popular and hammered copper sinks are also prime choice for the bathroom. The paper banners (they look a bit Nepalese) that you see hanging across streets or are used for decoration during parties or fiestas are called *Papel Picado*. Mexicans use multitudes of candles and you can find them in all shapes and sizes. Thinking of parties? They are often illuminated with *Luminarios,* wax-lights in brown paper bags that we also see used north of the border nowadays.

-0-0-0-0-

Arriving for the first time in Baja California

A short flight of about four hours from Vancouver, landed us just around midnight at a very new looking International Airport in San Jose del Cabo. A short drive later the taxi dropped us off at the lobby of our Hotel for the first week, right at the beach of the Sea of Cortes.

Going through our suit-cases to change clothes and to find sandals, I opened the balcony doors. The thunderous sounds were unbelievable. Scents, a mixture of herbs, flowers and salty air were just incredible. When I looked into the courtyard I saw it was full of at least one story tall cacti, blooming and giving us those wonderful scents mixed with the smell of the ocean. I peeked around the overhanging palapa to see if the sky was overcast because it sounded like thunder in the distance. But instead, I saw a splendid open sky full of bright stars making it clear to see lots of constellations.

We could not figure out where those enormous thunder-like sounds came from until we decided to go for a stroll along the gorgeous sandy beach. As tired as we were, we had to get a glimpse of our new surroundings. It must have been a windy day because we soon found out that it was the waves crashing on to this beautiful beach that made the loud sounds of thunder.

What else could it have been? We were in paradise, three hundred plus days a year of sunshine they say blesses this southern peninsula of Baja California. So, naturally, the next morning the first sun-rays came over the horizon and were so powerful, they literally burned us out of bed.

-0-0-0-0-

Surfing is popular in Mexico

As I have noticed an increasing number of younger people moving to Mexico, not necessarily to retire but to live and play here while maintaining a long-distance job that they can do from their new location. Some are finding locally existing needs and starting their own businesses while putting a fair amount of time in on the water. There are now so many forms of surfing. Wind-Kite and board surfing turning old communities into newer, exciting destinations.

The Mecca for kite- and wind surfing is on the East-coast of the southern Baja near Los Barriles, Buena Vista and a bit further north, at La Ventana. From December to March the winds are very predictable and strong any time after 10.30 or 11 O'clock.

At the other side of Mexico, Isla Blanca at the Riviera Maya, is the hot spot. In Yucatan there are Progresso and El Cuyo. Back on the West-coast, Bucerias at Riviera Nayarit has the winds later into spring. in May, Bucerias has the biggest kite-boarding event in Mexico, the 'Festival del Viento' where Pro kite boarders from all over Mexico and abroad come together and show spectacular kite-boarding.

For old fashioned board surfing, at Km. 57 on the Trans Peninsular highway in Baja Norte, and a bit further south at La Fonda are 2 good beach breaking surf spots in Baja California. All the way down the Baja coast, there are many more spots but often hard to get to. In Southern Baja, Zippers is one of several good waves in the San Jose del Cabo area. It's a reef break, breaking over cobblestones and sand. Suitable for beginners in smaller conditions, up to advanced surfers in larger, more powerful swells. 45 minutes up the coast from Cabo is Los Cerritos, with a left and right beach break and a mostly sandy bottom. It can get busy here at times. Good for beginners to intermediate. La Pastora, four km north of Todos Santos has a rocky bottom and is more suitable to intermediate and better.

The State of Nayarit, on the mainland Mexico Pacific side, has more then 11 surf spots. Dinosaur, La Bahia and San Blass beach are some of the best ones out there. A 'point break' at Punta de Mita is also considered a good one and not too crowded.

There are a more spots south to the state of Jalisco. On the Gulf-side there is not much of a great swell except for right and left beach break at Tampi near Vera Cruz.

-0-0-0-0-

After 25 Years .... camping again and hot springs

Home in Victoria, we had made the plan to kayak some of the wonderful nooks and inlets of the Bay of Conception. We had the charts, life jackets etc. except the kayak. The bad weather at time of departure had changed that and now we were going to rent one somewhere local. To do that, our best bet was the early morning, when the waters are still. The heat of the day almost guarantees strong winds towards the afternoon on a daily basis. Close to a launch spot and a rental facility, we found the beautiful beach at Camp Eco Mundo, an ecological responsible kayak center (no more) that recycles everything and operates strictly on solar-power.

The owners of the camp were back in California so all we had to communicate with was a Mexican girl who was in charge but didn't speak any English. When I asked if we could pitch our tent somewhere, she kept shaking her head and lured me to the half-open palapas with cots; bring your own linen. They were 12 US for the night. Then she took me to the 'Honeymoon suite'. It had something that had to function like a door and a double-size cot made-up with sheets and a large sleeping bag. It looked comfortable to me and the $ 20 would not have been a problem if we had set our minds on trying our new acquired tent and doing the real thing after 25 years.

What they call a 'honeymoon suite' was still a *palapa* with critters and dust but above ground and something to close the structure a bit from the elements and the outside world. Well the elements were in our favor today. Windy, but sunny and as soon as the sun sets, the wind would ease entirely, and a full moon would make this a night we would not soon forget.

Our three-person tent was purchased before we left for this adventure and while I was leaning toward staying in the honeymoon suite, my wife preferred our own tent and sleeping bag, resulting in me pitching the new tent for the first time. By now it was very windy, 25 knots and whitecaps. Deciding which location and direction to pick for the entrance was a crucial task. It turned out to be a lovely spot, slightly protected behind some low growing bush and only ten yards from the high-water line giving us the relaxing sound of the waves washing the white sandy beach. Once we had the inner tent up, we put the twin-size mattress and other stuff in it to keep the floor down in the wind. The mattress was inflated in two minutes with a 12-volt pump that works fast once you have found the right holes to plug into. The balance of our camping equipment had a lot to wish for, but we were going to try it anyway.

Once we were settled in, a lot of old memories came back to us. If the weather had been so nice as today, we would not have given up camping 25 years ago. But here, it is dry, the sun is out, no bugs to speak of and a beautiful private spot on the beach. This way it's an easy sport, because that's what it is, a sport. You are constantly busy, doing this, finding that, preparing for nighttime etc.

By 4 O'clock, the Mexican girl had left and closed the bar and store but also everything else. We had paid her $ 8 for camping with the idea to be able to use the facilities. Well, the water was cut off to a tittle little drizzle and the power had probably not been on all day, so everything was in the dark that night. Good that we had plenty of candles and a strong flashlight. A full moon came up by 10 giving us so much light, I could almost read by it outside. After an early supper, darkness fell quickly, and we took a stroll along the beach. Jazz, our Golden retriever, always attracts attention and when we met some gringos with dogs, the dogs had to sniff things out. So did the owners, by exchanging the usual questions; where you from, how long are you staying, where you are going next etc. I pointed to a row of stones on the beach that were half submerged in the water and that led to a stone circle further out. We talked about swimming naked under the full moon later tonight, but I said, better not there, it looks as if the stones hold a waste outfall in place from the Eco Mundo washrooms.

"No way," they assured us, "that is a natural hot-tub."

Apparently, there are hot springs here everywhere in the shallow waters. The stones are there to walk to it, and the circle keeps some of the hot water in and when it mixes with the sea, the temperature is perfect.

I couldn't believe it, so the daughter of one of the gringos that come here every year took me out to prove it. How ignorant and negative of me to think that the Eco campground would spoil the water. But then, the springs had no tell-tales, you saw no bubble, nor did they smell of sulfur, so who would expect this wonderful phenomenon right in front of our pitched tent? The guidebook surely never mentioned it. Anyway, this was a bonus, and when the tide went out we went back to the crater like circle of stones that had a diameter of about 18'. The water was as hot as our hot tub at home, but here it came with little fish jumping around, trying to get out of the pool. There were many other similar spots along this crescent beach and a really nice one, the daughter pointed out to me, was at the other end below the red roofed house on the cliff. We planned to visit that one tomorrow morning when we would have the kayak to go there.

Back by our tent, we watched the phenomenal clear sky with so many celestial signs, unusual for a city slicker. Too bad that with clear skies come cold nights. We were starting to shiver and went inside where we only had one blanket for the two of us. Earlier I brought the emergency pack that we have in the car. It has a flat-folded aluminum thermo sheet that we could put on top just in case. Inside however, with a fat candle burning and all the tent-windows shut, it was not too bad for a while. Once asleep, without moving much more and the candle off, it became fricking cold. Every so often, I woke up from loud bangs that echoed against the mountainsides. They came apparently from truck mufflers that had to shift down because of the sharp turn and descend into the corner of the bay. Most trucks must drive all night, during the day we hardly noticed this noise. Later on, we heard someone walking by the tent and I saw a bright light shining on the tent and my heart slowed down drastically. We wondered if this would be the moment we would be robbed.

"Put some money in a different spot, so they don't have it all when they take your wallet," my wife said in a soft voice.

"I think it is the security guard," that was what I was hoping for. Strangely enough, we had not seen or heard a guard before and it was now 4 am, the coldest time of the night that must have woken us. We went out for a pee, which was a wonderful experience as it was so bright with that enormous full moon reflecting on mirror like water in the bay.

Without further incidents, we made it through the night, close together, snuggled up to preserve body heat.

The next morning, tea was made and a plan for kayaking was worked out with the nautical charts I had had for Christmas. At 8 am, the *cantina* or bar opened up, not by the girl from yesterday, but by a retired gringo that just filled in for the day. We needed purified water, so I went to buy a bottle and to pick up some coffee at the same time.

"Well, I don't recommend the coffee," he said while sipping on one himself.

"They are out of coffee and all I found was some very old instant."

"Well than, I just take the water and would like to pay for a double kayak for the day. How much is that together?" I asked.
Even with the large chalkboard detailing all the prices, he could not figure out what I owed him. Anyway, I worked it out for him and paid him $ 25, got two paddles and went back to the tent to finish breakfast without coffee.

Fortunately, the tide had come in high so launching the long kayak was easy. We first went for the shaded, steep rocky hillsides, thinking the sun will be long enough burning down on us. If we can postpone that and still paddle around, that would be a bonus. The azure blue water was deep and clear and for a while, we didn't see much other than rocks and algae. But later, on southern exposed rocks and shore, some coral came into view with hundreds of fish that shot around like piranhas. Around the corner into the next bay, we went one further, so we could look at the popular Coyote beach. Then we turned north to go between some islands and came close to a cormorant colony. They were as tame as in the Galapagos Islands. They stayed where they were even though our paddles could reach them, just showing off their fine plumage, holding their wings wide in the air to dry.

A few hours later we landed on Playa Santispac, a beach north from where we started out. The clock was approaching eleven, a time that the wind usually picks up here and I kept a close eye on the water for that reason. Yesterday afternoon, when I put up the tent, it was white capping and we would not like to be trapped in a catchy situation like that. The spot where we landed was at the beginning of a mangrove with a fairly narrow entrance. The current was still going in strong when we landed. Ten minutes later as I kept watching for signs on the water, I noticed the tide had turned around already and was picking up remarkable speed in the opposite direction, the one we had to go. A bonus again, but what I didn't understand that there had been no slack. One moment the tide was going in strong, the next it was running out strong. Anyway, we enjoyed the ride and hugged the shore on the way back to our bay where several crater-like structures along the high-waterline were waiting to be explored.

We found the deeper, cemented-in hot spring and had to try it out of course. With the high tide filling it up with seawater, the temperature was still like the one at home, just around 104 degrees. We soaked for a while and rolled over the edge into the cold seawater. Fabulously refreshing! And back into the crater again to warm up and do the whole thing over again and again. Too bad we had to go back to our base, to pack, have lunch and move on.

Back at Eco Mundo, I handed the paddles to the old gringo, asked once more for coffee and when he had made us some after me begging for it, he closed the place down and we were on our own again. The kayak camp being ecologically friendly recycles all glass and plastic. Behind the huge bins where they collect all this stuff are some showers, a washroom and two sinks in the middle. For a shower, you had to pay extra to get a key, but you would expect the toilet to operate if you pay for camping. The toilet was built higher up, on a filthy, piss stained, wooden base of about 2 x 2 feet. Similar structures you used to find on Whistler Mountain, but there they are cleaned once or twice a day. Here the flush-handle didn't do anything and there was a little plastic hose with a spray handle that was supposed to do the job. First off, the handle was hanging down, just next to the bowl, so that anybody that does a stand-up job and does not aim well would spill over the handle. Secondly, when I got the courage to pick up the filthy handle, to get some water for our dog Jazz, pressing the nozzle did not amount to much. A small dripping spray occurred, and it took a sickening long time just to fill her small water-bowl. Now the problem was to make sure that it was not salt water pumped from to sea. Where was the cistern, or tank where this water came from? When I saw it on the roof of the structure, I put my finger in it and tasted it. It was not salty, but still, I could not put the image out of my mind of the millions of germs that must be flourishing on this hose sitting next to the toilet bowl in this hot climate. I tried to wash my hands by one of the sinks, but here again, water only dripped out, whatever I tried. With soap and patience, I did manage to clean my hands and wondered once more, what had we paid a camping fee for.

We had lunch and packed our gear while still enjoying some more of our wonderful surroundings. Some gringos were trying ancient surfboards in the bay, but the wind never picked up this day. By 2 pm we were on the road south to Loreto.

We did it! We camped on a beautiful beach, kayaked, and felt great, brave and accomplished.

-o-0-0-0-

Fiestas in Mexico

It is said that fiestas claim 317 days a year in the historic town of San Miguel de Allende. National holidays- and religious are only a small part of the mix. Every town has their own celebrations, often around their patron's day. Some are at the same time and others are at different times at different locations throughout Mexico. This means that at any given time, there is a fiesta going on somewhere in Mexico. Someone who checked this out, claims that there are only nine days left, that go without a fiesta somewhere in all of Mexico.
In the next couple of pages, you find a selection of some National fiestas, followed by non-National, regional fiesta.

Independence Day, Viva Mexico

For good reason, September in Mexico is called *Mes de la Fiestas Patrias,* month of national festivities and so after a long boring summer the fiesta scene is finally heating up. And so is everything else this time of year, the weather hot and humid, locals excited about their fiestas and gringos planning their return.

About a week prior to *Dia de la Indepencia* you may see many street vendors setting up shop at the busy corners all over town in preparation for the fiesta on September 16. This is considered the most important Mexican national holiday, equivalent to the 4th of July in the USA. And they are patriotic all right, the Mexicans, no less than gringos. Street vendors will be peddling besides the usual refreshments and snacks, all sorts of patriotic wares. This is a good time to buy national flags that are available in all sizes, streamers and even candies that are now in the important three national colors of red, white and green. Remember this; the colors all symbolize something different and represent important parts in the celebrations. The green, on the left side of the flag symbolizes hope and independence. The white section in the middle symbolizes religion and purity and red on the right, symbolizes union and the blood of the fallen national heroes.

On September 16, 1810 the rebellion started on mainland Mexico which eventually led to Mexico's independence from the 'mother-land' Spain. Be aware that this is a statutory holiday all over Mexico with banks and government offices closed.

Comparing the US Independence Day with Mexico's, you will notice that Mexicans are way more emotional than gringos. This huge fiesta is a two-day affair as the party always starts the evening before. That evening, it will be busy on the streets and you can feel the excitement building particularly in the centers of town, and around city hall. The climax is exact at 11 pm, when the Mayor will kick-start the party with the independence yell called *El Grito*, the start-sign for a patriotic party that can last all night long. Everyone will copy and will yell 'Viva Mexico' three times as loud as they can.

The most dramatic and impressive celebrations are held in Mexico City and in Dolores Hidalgo, the town where the reading of the Declaration of Independence originally took place. The leader of the independence movement was Father Hidalgo, the spiritual leader of Dolores. When he learned on September 15, 1810, that a conspiracy against the ruling Spanish had been discovered by the authorities, he had no choice but to start the rebellion. It was Hidalgo who rang the church bell and shouted the cry for independence. That very same bell is now on the balcony of the National Palace in Mexico City where the president commemorates this historic event every year. At 11 pm sharp Enrique Peña Nieto, the current President of the republic will ring this historic bell and will shout over the large *Zocalo* the names of the heroes of the revolution and ending with *"Viva*

Mexico" "Viva la independencia." The crowd, waiting in anticipation, echoes back as loud as they can *"Viva Mexico"* while the air fills with confetti, streamers and noise you cannot imagine. From all directions, paper *Castillos* explode in showers of red, white, and green, the national colors of course. This tradition is observed all over Mexico, with so much gusto throughout the night, that no one can escape this party.

Closer to home, patriotic Mexicans decorate their house for this occasion with flags in windows and put them on cars just as when their national soccer team was playing for the world-cup. No fiesta goes without traditional food. On the evening of September 15, Mexicans prepare a special corn-meal, *pozole* and *buñuelos*, and enjoy dinner together with the family before they go to the central square or municipal hall. In Baja's State capital of La Paz, colorful festivities are held in the center of town while everywhere else, the big event will be the parade on the morning of *Dia de la Independencia*. School kids, politicians and many people from different organizations will proudly parade through the streets.

Most larger towns organize fairs and rodeos that are great fun for all walks of life and can be a great opportunity for gringos to experience the Mexican spirit.

Food of course, is a major part of these festivities. Road stands will offer the traditional *antojitos*, strictly translated as 'little whims,' a tasty variety of small appetizers. A huge selection of Mexican candies can be found that could be washed down with *ponche*. This *ponche*, or punch, is made of fruits that are now in season: particularly guayabas, sugarcane, mango and apples. It has a delicious aroma.

Juarez Day, Mexican's greatest National Hero

He was the first indigenous president of Mexico and is celebrated every year as Benito Juarez Day on the third Monday in March. This is a statutory holiday, celebrated nationwide and employees are entitled to a day off with pay. Mexico has two more types of holidays, civic and religious or traditional festivities that do not qualify for a paid day off. Benito Juarez is an icon between many Mexican heroes and his birthday is not until March 21st but for him they made a special rule to celebrate his accomplishments on the 3rd Monday in March, always close to St. Patrick's Day on the 17th. This makes for plenty of opportunities to keep the liver wet during the parties that weekend. Keep in mind that banks and government offices will be closed on statutory holidays.

The fiesta starts in the morning with melodious parades through town while all day long you can find local food and interesting craft stalls on busy intersections and street corners. Juarez is one of Mexico's most celebrated heroes. Simply put it, Juarez is to Mexico what Abraham Lincoln is to the United States. Americans only called a few landmarks after their hero, but Mexicans took this much further and called a street after him in every town of the country, large or small. The Juarez holiday is a true fiesta for Mexicans of all ranks and for good reason as he had a very eventful life and was instrumental to what became of this country. He fought for Mexican independence, this time from France, not Spain. Confused enough? When there are Mexican history classes conducted, take them and check it out. Anyway, as a statesman, Juarez brought in huge reforms which was quite an accomplishment for an orphaned boy from a Zapotec Indian family. He grew up in the south as a shepherd and was basically illiterate until the age of twelve. He realized to become somebody; he had to move to the city. That is when he went to Oaxaca to educate himself. After learning the Spanish language, he became interested in law and politics. Before he even practiced law, he became a strong defender of Indian rights. And so, he became a lawyer, a judge and eventually the governor of the state of Oaxaca. There he got in a position to support the national legislation to confiscate all the land from the church. This was too liberal for the dictator at the time and poor Benny got expelled with a group of other similar intellectual rascals. He ended up in New Orleans for a while maintaining a living as a cigar factory worker.

With the Liberal movement in Mexico growing, Benito Juarez was eager to return to Mexico. And actually, with some support from the United States the tables were turned and the dictator by the quaint name of Santa Anna was sent into exile. Juarez became minister of the interior and he used his power to curtail the supremacy of the church even further. However, rocking that boat backfired badly. Another general led a coup, Congress was dissolved, and Juarez arrested. The general takes over the Presidency and as a counter move gives Juarez an out of jail card. It was just cat and mouse. Once Juarez got his freedom back, he might have celebrated with his friends by sipping a fine Bohemian cerveza because beer just became fashionable at that time.

A few years later Juarez got himself into a real pickle. During the bloody Reform War, Liberals fighting the Conservatives and vise versa, he was picked up by the General's forces and sentenced to be executed. He escaped the firing squad at the last minute thanks to intervention of the poet Guillermo Prieto, now another common street name. The short, stocky Juarez never gave up and came out on top as he eventually became the first indigenous President of the United States of Mexico. His office lasted for 14 years. Juarez was a progressive reformer and led the Mexican opposition against the French invasion, kicked the frogs out and with the help of a few conspirators, he had their puppet emperor Maximilian arrested and executed. Now more than two hundred years later, Mexico still celebrates Juarez's birthday with a national holiday. A good day to toast with a Mexican beer, any type you like.

Revolution Day

One of Mexico's proudest celebrations is *Dia de la Revolutión* which is officially celebrated on November 20. This was the start of a revolt against the established order in 1910 that turned into a messy civil war that lasted nearly ten years. Obviously Mexican society was a different ball of wax at that time. There was a 34-year dictatorial regime of General Porfirio Diaz, who had originally good intentions but turned out basically taking care only of a small upper-class establishment. During his dictatorship Mexico enjoyed political stability and grew in many areas. He created new industries and railroads, but the improvements didn't do anything for ordinary people and caused huge inequality between rich and poor. A few owners controlled most of the land and the masses of people had very limited rights which after long enough suppression were stirred into a wide uproar from the ordinary people of Mexico. A revolution does not come overnight. This one had been brewing for some time and on November 20, Francisco Madero who was an educated man, initiated a general strike and declared the electoral process under Diaz invalid. He got widespread support from the brave peasants from Peubla, Coahuila, Chihuahua and Sonora. And so, the revolution broke out, and for good reason. To have the same guy at the helm for 34 years would even make a donkey suspicious.

What followed was an intense struggle for power and democracy between leaders of which some became heroes at that time and are honored to this day with street names all over Mexico.

You might have recognized the name Madero, he was actually a pacifist, and needed someone to do the fighting for him. In the north, the infamous bandito Pancho Villa and his cronies were itching for a good fight. Instead of playing Robin Hood, as they had in the past, Villa joined the cause and led the revolution in *Del Norte*.

In the South Emiliano Zapata, took hold in the state of Morelos with the remarkable help of many Soldaderas, women solders. Perhaps the most popular Zapatista female soldier was Margarita Neri, who participated as a Zapatista commander. And, no, the famous margarita cocktail was not named after her. That's another story.

The following year, Madero was elected president, but not for long as he was captured by one of his own generals and soon after assassinated. Pancho Villa stayed in charge of the North and got help from Venustiano Carranza in the state of Coahuila and Alvaro Obregon from the Sonora district. The fighting went on for a few more years, giving Hollywood the idea to shoot a movie about it. So Pancho Villa became a movie star and revolutionary hero at the same time.

The Zapatistas took the land back from the estate owners, and divided it between the peasants, re-instating the ejido system which originated from the Aztecs. The struggle continued for years but eventually Carranza managed to survive the chaos and came out on top as *El Presidente* and developed the Constitution in 1917, the one that is still in effect today.

-0-0-0-0-

Other Fiestas

Semana Santa, **Holy week, Mexico's Prime Vacation Time**

Do you ever wonder why Easter is every year on a different date? Unlike most other fiestas that are on a set date, this one depends on the moon. The simple explanation is that Easter Sunday falls on the first Sunday after the full moon that follows the first day of spring. There is a more complicated version, but I want to save you from that. During Easter in Mexico, you don't want to go anywhere because it will be busy on the roads and accommodations are scarce or hard to find as most hotels are booked long in advance.

The week prior to Easter is called '*Semana Santa*' or Holy week which leads up to Easter weekend.

Easter in Mexico is like our 'spring break' except not just for the kids but the whole family celebrates. Thousands of people take the week before Easter off and if they are students or have a cushy government job, they take two weeks. Everyone is on the move, hotels are overbooked, and coastal areas are the most popular destinations, drawing the entire nation to the sandy beaches.

Why is Easter so popular in Mexico? If you take the church calendar, Easter is the most important fiesta of the entire year, more so than Christmas. And since 90 percent of the Mexican population is still Catholic; virtually the whole country celebrates it with an extended holiday. Another reason is that Easter is not just one day or a weekend. It is celebrated during that whole week of *Semana Santa* starting on Palm Sunday.

Palm Sunday is for a lot of Mexicans the beginning of their annual vacation period making this high-season anywhere in Mexico. There is no point trying to take the ferry from La Paz to the mainland during *Semana Santa* as they are always totally booked long in advance. People from the mainland will travel - en masse- to see family or come to coastal resorts to camp on the beaches for the occasion. Most Mexicans are traveling in cars and trucks that are packed to the rim with the whole family in the back and their belongings tied to the roof. Watch out for flying debris from oncoming cars that might land on the middle of the road.

Strict observing of the catholic tradition is tapering off every year but there is still the core of Mexicans that go several times to church during *Semana Santa* to find relief in the many spiritual happenings. There are some nostalgic rituals and religious processions that take place in many parts of Mexico, some with intense re-enactments of the last few days of Christ's life. Church statues will be cleaned and brushed up to be taken for a walk. It is a time of masochistic self-torture that went in the past sometimes to extremes. Strangely enough, it's the torturous crucifixion that seems to appeal to the people of this country most. Passion Plays are held all over the world, but the one in *Iztapalapa,* a working-class neighborhood on the outskirts of Mexico City, takes the cake and is an absolute spectacle. It all started after a horrible cholera epidemic that ended in 1833. The survivors organized the play out of gratitude that they were spared.

Nowadays over the duration of *Semana Santa*, two million people come out to watch this spectacle that has a cast of nearly 500 people. Yeah, nothing comes small in Mexico. Competition for the roles is intense and is taken very seriously by the candidates. The requirements of those who wish to play Jesus or Mary are especially strict. To assure a proper state of purity, tradition demands that neither be allowed to date, drink, smoke, or go to parties once they take on the role. More restrictions have been added recently: no tattoos or piercings. Candidates must also prove that they have the money to pay for the splendid costumes they need.

Whoever plays Jesus must be able to bear a ritual whipping in the square, then carry a cross weighing more than 200 pounds three miles and up a steep hill, where he has to endure a brief but real crucifixion in which he is bound to the cross for about 20 minutes.

The Judas role comes with a different kind of sacrifice. It is not just that he is the bad guy. In the *Iztapalapa* version, Judas ends up hanging himself out of remorse for having betrayed Jesus. Alfonso Reyes, a taxi driver who has played Judas in recent years said in an interview "So far, I haven't been the victim of physical aggression, but you're always anxious and uneasy because people are really transformed by this spectacle." When people in the audience shout "traitor" at you, the role can become quite humiliating especially when people get carried away and start pelting Judas with rotten fruit and other objects.

On Maundy Thursday, *Jueves Santo*, people all over Mexico, visit the churches. Wild chamomile and bunches of salvia are spread on the marble floors filling the churches with marvelous scents. People prepare themselves for the big day, Good Friday. This is unmistakably the highlight of the week, called *Viernes Santo* with many a procession through the towns again. Personally, I love this day because it is the quietest day in the neighborhood; all construction is at a complete standstill.

On Holy Saturday, Lent is over with a bang. Forty days of fasting since Carnival have come to an end and that is a good excuse for a party. In many mainland towns, Judas-figured fire-crackers blast the sky, church bells toll and large *papier-mâché* eggs filled with colorful confetti will burst and spread their vivid content all over the place. For gringos, it is time to see what the Easter-bunny has come up with. A fine bottle of aged tequila or a couple of six-packs would be just fine. *Felices Pascuas*, Happy Easter.

A most traditional fiesta, *Dia De Los Muertos,* Day of the Dead

Watch out for late October because many skeletons come out of the closet in Mexico. As Halloween is around the corner, you will see a lot of skeleton figurines, skulls and whatnot at bakeries, store windows and public places. But in Mexico, they have nothing to do with Halloween. They are part of a very traditional Mexican celebration called *Dia De Los Muertos,* Day of the Dead which is two days after Halloween.

In ex-pat areas you nowadays see more announcements for Halloween parties then for Day of the Dead as Mexican culture, particularly around gringo communities is changing rapidly. Particularly the children in those gringo communities seem to reap the fruits of Halloween, candies in this case, and who can blame them. As Halloween is a secular festivity that comes with funny or scary masks, skeletons and lots of candy, it can easily be confused with items from the traditional Mexican celebration of *Dia De Los Muertos* on November 2. However, it is a good thing that Halloween despite becoming increasingly more popular throughout Mexico, does not diminish the celebration of Day of the Dead.

During the last week of October preparations for Day of the Dead are all around you. Watch for little displays in shops, public places and at home as most Mexicans participate in preparations for *Dia de los Muertos.* This event is poorly understood by us gringos but quite fascinating and colorful never the less. Go and check out the offerings exhibited in public places such as libraries, cultural centers.

Day of the Dead is a time to reflect on the meaning of life. For gringos it is amazing to see how Mexicans handle the process of mourning. They use a lot of attributes as you will see at the little altars that sprout up around town which make this tradition quite fascinating. Locals are buying the special velvety purple coxcombs and the strong smelling Marigolds that are for sale at flower stalls. They use them to decorate the special altars that are set up for this occasion in the home or office. What is particularly eye catching and shocking at the same time for gringos is the macabre selection of candies. You will see skeleton lollipops and chocolate skulls for sale on street corners and at bakeries. You might pass on them, but kids love them. Typical *Pan de Muerto,* a sugared bread roll, fragrant with orange peel and anise and with crossed 'bones' of dough on top is also part of the celebration. All these items go to the altar or are brought to the grave-site of the deceased loved one, sometimes already on the eve of November 1st. Often the family will add a photo of the individual and brings fruit, incense and candles. They might also put a bottle of the deceased's favorite drink at the grave-site and if she or he smoked, a pack of cigarettes. Day of the Dead celebration is of course a personal affair. We can watch quietly from a polite distance but please don't take photographs at cemeteries.

Knowing some background of *Dia de los Muertos*, makes it much better to understand. It's an ancient tradition originated by the Aztecs and Mayas, mixed with Spanish- Christian influence. The early Aztec and Mayan Indians had a happy disrespect for mortality, something that was perhaps acquired with a strong belief in reincarnation. With solid faith in that, maybe the whole affair starts to make more sense.

A very popular creation around Day of the Dead is the figurine of Catherina, the skeleton lady with the big hat. A few years ago I ran into some new variations on her theme. Skeleton ladies with wings, referring to butterflies, one of the creatures Aztecs believed they would reincarnate in. Another new character on the block of the large variety of skeleton figurines was Michael Jackson in his characteristic jacket. Maybe David Bowie and Prince will be next.

As the Aztecs believed that one day we all come back as hummingbirds or monarch butterflies, the rituals during *Dia De Los Muertos* are designed to attract the spirits from their loved ones back home. Wouldn't it be spooky if a hummingbird would fly by the graveyard or near the house that night? Apparently, this is not uncommon as I have heard from my Mexican friends. Even without hummingbird fly-bys, the whole affair of sitting around a graveyard all night must be quite creepy and nerve-racking for gringos. Perhaps we should try to be more like the Aztecs and open up to the idea of reincarnation. What is wrong with coming back as a hummingbird or a butterfly as long as some caring human fills the feeder with red margaritas or aged tequila.

Radish Night, or *La Noche de Rábanos*

Perhaps the shortest fiesta in Mexico and not even celebrated nationwide, but it's true to its name, as the Radish Night festival lasts only a few hours for the simple reason that vegetables have a pretty short lifespan as folk art.

This unusual event is held each year in the old *zocalo* of the city of Oaxaca and starts at sunset on December 23. It is of particular interest to folk-art aficionados who should put it on their Mexican bucket list because it is not an overstatement to say that it's one of the most unusual folk-art competitions in all of Mexico.

Now keep in mind that the radishes in Oaxaca are not the little red round ones that you see in your regular supermarket. They are thick, long and cylindrical, measuring up to 20 inches and weighing up to seven pounds. The city of Oaxaca has allocated a special area near El Tequio Park to grow the monster radishes for the event under strict supervision. They are obviously no good for consumption as they use chemicals and strong fertilizer while keeping them much longer in the ground, way after the normal harvests, to allow them to reach monumental sizes with all sorts of freakish appendages.

This seems to arouse incredible inspiration in Oaxaca's carvers, who will use the morphed shapes to their advantage and hope to come up with a winning radish. The stakes are high as the winner takes home 15,000 pesos and his picture in the morning paper.

Radishes are originally from China, but in 16th century colonial Mexico, radishes and other vegetables were introduced by the Spanish. Oaxaca's carving tradition goes back a long time and specializes in wood. Farmers began carving radishes into figurines and other subjects as a way to attract customers' attention during the Christmas market which was held in the main square on December 23. The formal competition dates back to 1897 and now has prizes in various categories.

Night of the Radishes has become very popular and attracts over 100 contestants and thousands of visitors. Relating to the time of year, carvings represent anything from animals, saints and dancers to the Virgin Mary. The humble red skin radishes have a nice softer and contrasting white inside which is very adaptive to intricate sculptures. Some carvers peel the red skin and use it as draped clothes or flags. The inventiveness of the contestants is endless. The problem however is that radishes will soon wilt after cutting. Therefor the creations can only be displayed for a few hours. This has led to very long lines for those wishing to see the works.

Last December, 94 carvers competed in the adult categories, along with 61 youth and 50 children. They register months in advance and the radishes are handed out on December 19. Then they have three days to work out a plan or design and the actual carving will take place on the 23rd, before the results are displayed at sunset. The ahhh's and oohh's float in the air as the crowds take in the exhibition slowly walking by. Even the most diligent spraying of the radishes cannot prevent the masterworks from browning and wilting in the warm Oaxaca night. Therefor the winners will be announced around 9 pm under a sea of flashing cameras. Soon the shortest fiesta in Mexico winds down and people will drift off to other booths to sample some of the many sweets and pastries made especially for the Christmas season. Strangely enough, Radish Night has not caught on anywhere else in Mexico.

Villista Cavalcade Fiesta

There is a time of year that National or religious fiestas are as scarce as there are bottles of beer left in my fridge after a long weekend. That is when they make up some secular fiestas, just to have fun or to pump money into the local economy.

A truly Mexican fiesta in mid-summer is *Villista Cavalcade,* a week-long fiesta around mid-July. It's held in Chihuahua, capital of the Mexican state by the same name, to commemorate the assassination of that revolutionary rascal *Pancho Villa*.

Who has not heard about *Francisco "Pancho" Villa*, the leading figure in the 1910 Mexican Revolution? "Of all Mexican Revolution leaders, no one was as controversial as *Francisco Villa*" according to *Jorge Carrera*, president of the Chihuahuan Culture Institute. *"No one has remained as strongly in people's memory as he has."* Perhaps his importance is fading now that "the short one, *El Chapo*' was captured in early 2016. But that is another story. This *Villista Cavalcade* fiesta attracts many performances of classical and folk music and groups of minstrels strolling through the historic center of Chihuahua. However, the absolute highlight of the fiesta is the *cavalcade* itself, a parade on horseback from the city of Chihuahua to Hidalgo del Parral, some 136 miles away, where *Pancho's* assassination took place. Since its first occurrence, this rambunctious cavalcade has grown progressively larger. Over 1,000 horseback riders are expected to participate and about 400 motorcyclists are joining the fun in recent years. Can you imagine the dust? A hankie for your face might come in handy and don't forget a few six-packs to quench the thirst.

Getting there can be an adventure by itself. Not so much if you simply take a plane, but if you like me, take the ferry north from La Paz across the Sea of Cortez and go over land, it will be. Prepare for a choppy boat ride to Topolobampo, then a fast taxi into Los Mochis where you buy a ticket for that famous '*Chepe*' train ride, right through the massive Copper Canyon district to Chihuahua. This is an absolutely spectacular trip and worth every peso.

Think about this for a moment: going to celebrate an assassination. Isn't that what we love about Mexico? No scruples with mortality. Remember 'Day of the Death' in November? Anyway, *Pancho's* assassination actually happened on July 20, 1923 and only in Mexico, this calls for a boisterous party. Perhaps it is just smart thinking on the part of the tourist office in Chihuahua where they only two decades ago came up with this fiesta to honor *Francisco Villa*. His death is reconstructed every year on the exact spot where it happened.

Re-enactments are popular in Mexico and as if there are not enough casualties in the northern States in real life, a few dressed-up characters as *Pancho* and his cronies get a number of rubber bullets fired into them when they appear in their 1919 Dodge sedan from around a corner.

Pancho's body took the brunt of the assault and died almost instantly while his hands were reaching for his gun. His skull was robbed from his grave and is still missing but the original Dodge is in the local museum where you can put your fingers in all the bullet holes from that day in 1923.

If you ever make it to Chihuahua, *Pancho's* former classy residence is turned into that museum where the Dodge is displayed in the courtyard. It's really worth a visit and why not combine it with a clamorous party at the same time?

Carnival in Mexico

This is a wonderfully free-spirited event in many larger towns across Mexico. Some years it is an early 'Carnaval' as they like to call it here. 'Carnaval' comes from the word '*carne*,' meaning meat, last of the meat that is. As one is supposed not to eat any meat for 40 days, the period of Lent. And then, before you know it, it's Easter Saturday, when the butcher will be busy again.

The carnival parades have a different theme each year. A while ago in La Paz the theme was *"Plumajes Ancestrales"* or "Ancestral Plumage." It was a beautiful parade with many extravagantly dressed-up ladies showing feathers all over their gorgeous bodies. If you were lucky enough to be in La Paz at the right time, you have a good idea now what Mardi Gras is like. Here in Mexico however, it is a peaceful event, unlike the glamour and killings in Rio or New Orleans.

Problems and worries are washed away for a while and you can make friends for life. Carnival can release huge amounts of stress and is over too quickly before reality stares you in the face again. Once the folks are back to work, they will be saving up all year to spend it all again in next year's five days of exuberant carnaval.

Alleyway parties, or *Callejoneadas*

Callejoneadas are a traditional form of nightlife for which folks come out to dance, sing and drink *mescal* or beer-based punch called *"heribertas,"* all for little money, almost free. According to tradition, this type of street parties started by a college student named Heriberto, whose last name has evaporated by country wide memory loss. Which happened perhaps by drinking too much *heribertas. Callejoneadas* were most commonly held at the end of the school year, but there is no specific reason needed to hold one. This is where we can learn from. In Zacateras, that famous historic city on Mexican's mainland is quite into *callejoneadas*. They form in front of the Palacio de Gobierno, where a *"tambora"* band or any type of musicians form a group of revelers. Besides the music, a key thing is that they have a painted or decorated donkey carrying jugs of *"heribertas."* After a while the party winds its way around the narrow streets and alleys of the city with people drinking *heribertas* from little jars called *jarritos.*

Now as it happens, that same colonial Zacateras on the mainland has a huge annual fiesta called *La Morisma* (the Moors). In the Nahuatl language, Zacateras means 'place where *zacata*, or grass is plenty.' During that fiesta it will be *cerveza* and tequila flowing plentiful and there will be lots of munchies to go with it because the annual fiesta *La Morisma* is a most spectacular, unimaginable eye-popping event.

It is held always on the last weekend in August and it might be of dubious historical significance, but if you can handle crowds, *La Morisma* is an awesome colorful spectacle to experience. Generations of families, from babies to grandpas and grandmas take part in the various troops that represent the Christians and the Moors that will ultimately reenact some medieval battles from Europe. While the original skirmishes happened centuries ago in

Spain, thousands of people are attracted every year to put on heavy war gear, old weaponry and helmets to go to the hills of *Bracho,* the local mound, to parade, fight a little bit and show off. *La Morisma* is mainly an open-air event of festivities that include various mock battles acted out in elaborate costumes and are encompassed by loud playing bands on each side of the battle ground. So, imagine the spectacle from war reenactments with no less than five thousand people dressed up in extreme colorful war-gear that charge up the mountainside. Before this outburst of power, huge parades of all the factions will march thru the town's center. Last year 10,000 combatants of all ages, males and females from all walks of life joined in the skirmishes. All the local horses must be out there as there is plenty of cavalry between the crowds with guns and swords making for exciting photo ops. *La Bracho* is the neighborhood where it all takes place and is within walking distance of the center of Zacateras. While the Moors and Españoles from out of town usually camp out on the hills during the festival, you might want to find accommodation in the historic town before you go.

This visually rich spectacle would not be complete without fireworks and smoke as it commemorates the battle of Lepanto in 1571. The original battle consisted of a fleet of the Christian alliance manned by 12,920 sailors and in total there were almost 28,000 fighting troops destroying the fleet of the Turkish Ottoman Empire.

Morisma Festival is one of the bigger annual Mexican traditions you don't want to miss if you can handle big crowds. Zacateras is a fine historical city worth a visit anyway.

One hundred years ago, during the revolution, Zacateras was at the center of attention when it was taken by the merciless troops of Francisco (Pancho) Villa. Ever since, the city has been a magnet of cultural activities and has preserved a splendor of beautiful architecture. In 1993, the historic center of the city was pronounced a UNESCO site. Imagine a full out party in this impressive colonial city. If you haven't put a tour to Mexico's colonial cities on your bucket list, do it now. Absolutely worth a trip!

Snorkeling and diving

Mexico has many good diving and snorkeling places. One of the best is off the east-side of the southern Baja Peninsula at Cabo Pulmo. The reef just about 100 yards off the shore of Cabo Pulmo, is a huge preserved area in the Sea of Cortez. It is world-famous for its splendor and large variety in fish and coral. On the Mexican Gulf side, the Island of Cozumel was an absolute high-light when I dove there. Guess, divers usually know their favorite destinations, so I will leave it at that.

One popular destination out of Cabo is Santa Maria's cove. This beautiful crested cove has reefs at both ends where the waves break, and the snorkeling is at its best. The temperature can be a bit on the cool side, but the variety of fish and coral is not bad. There isn't much shade here, so we rented an umbrella for a few hours. Then the crowds came in and with them the local merchants.

"Special price for you."

"Wanne look at my junk?"

"T-shirts or hats?"

A short while later they came with eatables, fruit, drinks you name it, and we almost found a need for something, "What about two Corona," I asked.

"No Signor, no beer on beach."

What nonsense that is! Next time we know now what to bring, and a sign to put up saying "we don't buy anything, Thanks for not disturbing".

I do give them credit for ingenuity and persistence however. The way they stack all their merchandise from the hips up or hang it all on sticks carried over their shoulders. Always trying and always coming back half an hour later just in case you have changed your mind.

Turtles Release in Todos Santos

Independent of the weather, every evening during winter at the beach in Las Tunas, a short drive north of Todos Santos, a small crowd gathers to participate in the release of about 100 baby turtles.

Yes, you read this right: this amazing event is happening almost on a daily basis from November to February. At sunset, the Tortugueros Las Playitas (a volunteer organization) releases about 100 turtle hatch-lings on the beach making the little creatures find their way to the Pacific Ocean, if they like it or not. The Todos Santos group patrols a stretch of about 22 miles of beach from Todos Santos to Las Playitas and the small community of Aqua Blanca to the north. A team of full-time individuals assisted by many rotating volunteers watch for trails and marks of fresh nests overnight and bring the eggs to the incubating greenhouse where the success rate of hatching increases from 50% to 80%.

I was watching the release of 100 'Golfinas' the other day. Olive Ridley turtles take anywhere between 45 to 60 days to hatch. In the greenhouse the eggs and hatch-lings are protected from cars or ATV's driving the beach, wild dogs roaming around and poachers. Turtle eggs are considered an aphrodisiac by Mexicans and seem to taste delicious, so you can see the controversy for an environmentally responsible approach. I was talking to a volunteer, an enthusiastic girl in her early twenties who took a week off work from her job in Mexico City to be here on the beach volunteering mainly evenings and nights. At night she is going on patrol with German (pronounce Jermane) Agundez, one of the full-time workers at the incubation station. With a bit of luck, they might find the nest of a Pacific Leather-back that has been on the beach already 3 times and is expected to drop her 4th batch tonight. This must be very exciting when you realize that Leather-backs grow over 6' long and weigh over 1000 pounds.

When the sun had sunk in the ocean and darkness set in, I tried to imagine what it would look like in the middle of the night, when a 1000-pound turtle clambers out from the surf onto the beach and shuffles up to the higher, dry section on the sand and starts digging a hole to drop her eggs into. Spooky, mystical and fascinating at the same time, particularly if you keep in mind that this majestic turtle was here before, long before I came to this beach. They can live up to 100 years and typically return every two-three years to lay eggs on the very beach where they once hatched.

Nature sure has its ways, and now I am looking at the release of 100 baby turtles that are a bit reluctant to take the plunge but eventually are swept away by the waves from the upcoming Pacific. They flutter their front wings and tumble around like they are thrown into a giant washing machine. It seems cruel, the poor things are released the same day they hatch. But that's what they would do anyway if they were not protected. The difference is that their numbers are much higher since these were protected in the incubating greenhouse that has been set up just behind the dunes at the *bocana* in Las Tunas.

I asked the lady in charge what their survival rate is once they are in the ocean and she told me only 1 in 500 seem to make it back as an adult. The couple that run the turtle program here are the owners of La Sirena Eco-Adventures, a Baja company that specializes in environmentally friendly activities like whale

watching, fishing, kayaking, hiking, and other outdoor activities. They have a federal permit to locally collect and rescue the eggs and release the hatch-lings of Olive Ridley, Black, and the massive Pacific Leather-back sea turtles along the stretch of beach in Todos Santos. They can use your help, and they invite serious volunteers to ride along with their biologists as they rescue and relocate turtle nests to the world's only Incubation Greenhouse right here in Todos Santos. This Eco Adventure could be your experience of a lifetime. As a volunteer you are trained in collecting data on nesting sea turtles, nest relocation, incubation greenhouse operation, nest excavation, and hatch ling releases. Early morning patrols are run on ATV's, evenings are spent releasing hatch-lings, and days can be spent supervising the incubation area, helping with beach clean-ups. For contact email tortugueroslasplayitas@gmail.com To plan a trip to the incubation greenhouse you should know some 'Baja Turtle Facts.' The nesting season for Olive Ridleys is from July through November. Black Turtles, a smaller, darker version of the Green Turtle, nests from August through January, and the Pacific Leather-backs come to the beach between October and April. Keep in mind that incubation takes anywhere from 45 to 78 days depending on the type of turtle. The hatchlings are only ready 45 -78 days after the nesting. Check them out on Facebook and be part of this ecological friendly and educational event free of charge. Donations to keep up materials and equipment are of course welcome and can be made on the spot.

-0-0-0-0-

Whale Watching near Guerrero Negro

There are several good places for whale watching in Mexico. Most are on the Pacific coast of Baja California. On our way south, we stopped halfway down the Baja, right at the border of North and Southern Baja where Pacific time zone changes into Mountain time at Guerrero Negro, at small industrial town.

At 8 am, we left in a small bus with 12 other gringos of which two were a typically gay couple, both hairdressers living in Tijuana but working in San Diego. Imagine the daily commuting over that busy border crossing! They were funny and had the right attitude to deal with that.

The bus took us all the way through town towards the salt-pans and shipping area where the salt is collected and the docks are. The salt storage is in huge piles, mountains, that look as white as alpine ski hills, complete with avalanche tracks from salt that has slid down the slopes.

Just past the salt-barges, two *pangas* were ready to take us out on "Scammon's Lagoon." A twenty-five-minute ride at full-speed got us to the first group of Gray whales. They are very common here in January and February and can amount to about 2000 at a given time in the lagoon. There supposed to be four baby whales in the bay, but we didn't see any that day. Instead, we saw several groups of very active, sexually active, whales. Usually five to seven whales of which one or two were clearly female, smaller, and were humped several times by the large bulls. The satisfaction must have reached sensational proportions to the result that some whales breached free from the water out of exultation. Imagine, 35 tons of mass jumping out of the ocean! Thanks god, we were at a respectable distance.

On the way back, we finished prepackaged lunches that were provided and watched immense large salt-barges moving by. Empty ones being pushed back fast, for miles to the loading dock and full ones pulled slowly out into deeper ocean waters to be transferred over to deep-sea cargo ships. By noon, we were back at our motel, changed into shorts and walked our dog.

More Whale Watching

This time at Puerto Lopez Mateos, a small town on the Pacific side, which is a popular place to watch whales. A potholed, cracked road for the last 30 km brought us to a dusty, dirty little town where all the action was past the town, by the pier and waterfront. "Whale Fiesta" was on and a loud mariachi band made sure you could hear them from all over the village.

On this sunny, but windy afternoon we could see whales from the pier. It's on a narrow bay, and the amazing thing was to see tails and sprays everywhere you looked. We were not dressed warm enough to charter a boat right then. The plan was to stay overnight and charter a *panga* tomorrow morning for a few hours and then go on our trip further south.

The next morning, we had hoped to find mirror-like water, early in the morning, ideal for whaling and photography. But no, it was not going to be that easy.

The wind was still blowing making if very cold and now there was a dark overcast with a possible rainstorm starting any time soon. With ski-underwear, all the sweaters and hats, gloves and jackets we could find, we arrived at the pier at nine, negotiated for a while and got a deal on $ 100 for two hours. Still, I thought, that's much more than the going rate for a tramp in this neck of the woods, I am sure. Yesterday this bargaining wouldn't have worked, but today with the bad weather and Super Bowl on TV, they were scrambling for business.

Our skipper's name was Hector, an older fellow that knew what he was doing. However, as soon as we spotted a whale, he took his *panga* to that location, and the whale never showed up any more. He suggested going a bit further. He did that four times and by now we reached the opening from the Pacific into the lagoon, the only place where the whales could get in and out. A sure thing, but unlike yesterday when we could see them from the pier, now at about 10 km out, a good show still had to start while we were 45 minutes into the trip.

Then, suddenly, here they were! Huge sprays on all sides of us. A few males were doing wild things, but we saw more mothers and for the first time up close, with calves. They were so playful and never far apart from each other. A big spray soon followed by a smaller, then the torso, graciously moving like a wave just above the water and then the smaller baby's body coming up and moving down into the water. We were now very close to a remote yellow sandy beach at the north-arm of the lagoon.

There was one tent pitched, and the couple that camped there just woke up and started a ferocious morning exercise, surely to warm up. The sun had come out, but it was still cold. There was no more than two to three hundred meters between us and the beach, and in between, were the whales dolling around, sometimes breaching or popping up their head and spying around.

At the opening to the Pacific there must have been a dangerous reef, as breakers were reflecting now with white foam showing beautifully against a stark blue sky. It turned out to be a great whale show and we got back at the pier by 11, just as planned. At the motel, we changed in lighter clothes, walked the dog and went on our trip further south.

-0-0-0-0-

Car wash in Loreto

We went to the car wash with the idea to do it ourselves. Where did we get this stupid idea from? It would have been quite an undertaking. Hair from our dog has had almost two weeks to work itself all over our Volvo making it a filthy mess and the outside was very muddy from bad weather up north.

The concept of doing it yourself is not known here we found out, so instead, we had it done. We left the car with a price fixed at 60 pesos (40 for inside, 20 outside) and the agreement to pick the car up in an hour. So quick, in and out, that lowered my expectations drastically. Mind you, 60 pesos in an hour is not cheap in Mexico, depending on how many cleaners are going to do the job.

Once we left the car, all sorts of things were spinning through my head. I thought I was smart by taking the keys out the ignition and the spare keys from the side pocket. But at the same time, I forgot that my wife's wallet was somewhere below the seats. All sorts of equipment, spare parts, tools, beach chairs etc. were left in the car and I could only hope that everything would still be there when we would come back. They could tow the entire car away for what I knew, because we didn't stick around. I should have stayed and brought a book or something to do and watched our valuable car. But we had shopping to do and went to a pharmacy to pick up some Metacam for our dog that we had ordered the day before. We did groceries and got some liquor. Not an easy task at '*El Pescadero*', the local supermarket' with its poor selection of beer and wine. When I asked for a specialty store that might have Dos Equis Amber, they looked at me as if I was crazy. The shopkeeper pointed to the green labeled 'Special Lager' and apparently had never heard of Amber. I said "*negra*, like Negra Modello," in the cute, fat short bottles with the gold-foil necks. He gave up on me and I tried again somewhere else. No luck. The same for red wine. The one grocery store that is reasonable with the white wines and even had some imports, has no red other than the 'Padre Kino', the 9% one-liter bottles, light table wine that is sweet. Not really a drinkable delight.

When we came back by the car-wash an hour later, the young lad was still busy with the interior. My wife took a coffee while waiting and after that was finished she decided to walk home. I estimated the job to take another hour at least with the speed he was going. By now two guys were working on it and when they were done with the interior, I put our groceries inside and was pleasantly surprised with its cleanness. However, the precision they took on the outside of the Volvo would indicate another hour at least. At some point, four men were working away at it until a dirty police car drove up and two guys moved over to that car. The young lad that had started the job could not get enough of our car. He kept polishing and buffing away at it. He was a lightly built sixteen-year-old, polite and with a clean haircut wearing a yellow T-shirt. The other fellow who specialized in tire cleaning and everything around the wheels, was heavy set, with baggy jeans hanging about two inches below the onset of his butt and wore a black toque. That reminded me of how cold the wind was today.

While waiting, I had taken a seat on a red plastic Coca Cola chair at the taco stand next door. Past 11.30, workmen started to drop in for lunch all munching on a bowl of stew and beans as far as I could tell and one after the other ordered a bottle of pop. More tables were filling up and I started to feel uncomfortable sitting by one table and not ordering anything than the coffee from an hour ago. But I was not going to have lunch at a taco stand as of yet. Maybe at some later date but not today.

At one point I walked up to the Volvo and told the lad in yellow that he had done a great job. Please take my tip so I can get home for lunch before I faint.

When I opened the left side rear door, to see if my steering lock and other tools were still there, I saw to my shock my wife's wallet on the backseat. Wooh! Let's see if everything is still in there. As I didn't want to do this in view, I drove off and around the corner I looked inside to find to my relief that the Canadian Cash and all her credit cards were untouched. A truly feel-good experience, a place to recommend. They are right next to the Pemex gas station on the main drag into town.

The Mission of St. Javier (before they put in a new road)

For more than one reason, we planned today to drive the rough road into the mountains to the Mission of St. Javier. It's only 35 km off the highway but will take an hour and a half to two hours depending on your driving style. Why rush it? Also, the Sunday night will be very noisy again on the *Malecón* where we are staying. So why don't we pack some basics and stay overnight at the Mission? OK, some extra packing, including the cooler so we had some food in case we would run out or the local restaurant is closed.

For the first five km, the road is wide and gains altitude very gradually, so a good speed is possible. Once the road starts to climb, it gets narrow and snaking. The rocky- Sedona-like mountains turn from a gray, yellow to a beautiful tone of rusted red and orange. Driving away from shore, there are limited opportunities to look back and below to the azure blue waters of the Sea of Cortez. When we get a chance, we pull over and take-in the awesome views over the rough and desolate landscape towards the sea. There seems to be a lot more climbing to do as we see the hairpins glued to the side of the mountains ahead of us. I wonder where the pass will be that will take us beyond the first row of mountains into the interior.

It gets noticeably dryer, the few trees that were around change into shorter shrubs and later there is just soil and rock left.

Cliffs on both sides of us, one deep down and one steep up on the side my wife wants me to stick to with the car. Halfway, we stop at a small chapel across from the only ranch we have seen for over 10 miles. Here we are on a sort of plateau. The road stays narrow, not as much climbing any more but we must get through creeks and small river-beds four or five times. At last, there is a y-intersection where we are supposed to keep left and find the landscape getting greener and lusher again.

There was no sign of reaching the village nor the mission but being the only settlement of any size that we had seen for the last two hours, we assumed we made it. Suddenly we notice electric wires running through the valley and at the end; there is a massive stone church where we park the car under one of the few sizable trees good enough for some shade.

It is Sunday afternoon, and we are the only ones visiting this remote place until an hour later when we hear another car driving up to the village. We had hoped to find a restaurant and accommodation for the night. By the entrance to the main street, there was a man working his garden and we approached him with the question of a room for the night. "Si Si," and he pointed out of the village, past the Mission-church and mentioned the name Lourdes Correrez.

We drove off in that direction but were soon out of the village on a dead-end road. We had seen some primitive shacks and huts, nothing that resembled a hotel of some sort. In the village however, was a place that called itself a motel, but it was closed.

Again, we approached a man and he sends us in the same direction out of town. I asked him to come with us. He liked that, a ride in a luxury car and you could see him liven up and smile when I opened the car-door for him. He directs us to the simplest farm-like property at the edge of town. Chickens fleeing away in all directions as we drive up to a hut that had to be the house of

Lourdes. Kids in dressed and undressed state crawled out of all corners and stood gaping at us, the car and our dog. It became clear that Lucia had the keys to the one and only motel in the village and she stepped also in the car and with the four of us now, we went back to the motel in town. She showed us the smallest room first. They were in detached, stone and clay structures of two under one palapa roof. No indoor plumbing, no chairs, very little light and she was asking $ 35 for a night! No kidding. Not getting an enthused response, she showed us the larger unit, which had an indoor bathroom and was actually rustic and nice enough for me to spend the night, but my wife brought me back to my senses.

"What are we going to do here until tomorrow morning?" she asked.

The restaurant was an ordinary, cafeteria-style place with everything plastic and no patrons. We ordered some freshly made quesadillas and a Pacifico out of the fridge, no glass, for about 50 pesos. I could not picture me eating dinner here tonight and have fun with it. We thanked Lucia and the man that had brought us in contact with her and went next door where an older fellow was eager to show us his garden where he had sweetened grapefruits and other fruits that he grew in his yard.

The Mission built in 1597 was a quiet and mystical place where an irrigation system of small canals, something we had seen before in Todos Santos, made everything so lush and beautiful.

To make it back in good time to Loreto before dark, we left for the long bumpy road down to the coast. It was good to do this on a sunny day. If it would have been overcast, we could have been driving through clouds and everything would have looked scary and depressing. Now the lowering light set the rock formations in a blazing red with stark blue sky and magnificent ocean in the backdrop. Back in Loreto, at the *Malecón* the noisy traffic was already building.

"We could have missed this rambunctious traffic if we had stayed at the mission," I said to my wife. Poor woman, she shivered just by the thought of it.

-0-0-0-0

The hyper policeman in San Miquel de Allende

From our place on *Calle Quebrada* it was only a five-minute walk to the Teatro or Bellas Artes. But not without danger by being run over by the many buses with awfully smelly exhaust fumes. Early evening, strings of people are walking the narrow, uneven and often broken up narrow sidewalks.

Locals and gringos all going someplace, usually in opposite directions, with complete different goals in mind.

At one point we always had to cross the busy intersection at Zacateros and Canal Street, which is regulated by this hyper, but funny policeman. He orchestrates the traffic not only with his busy arm movements and hand signals but has a whistle constantly in his mouth through which he makes the funniest sounds. He practically speaks through his whistle and you better obey his signals or else he would fly off the handle.

-0-0-0-0-

Copper Canyon Adventure, Barranca del Cobre

One morning in March, we took the *Chihuahua El Pacifico* a train that connect the inland city of Chihuahua with the Pacific coast and runs along the Copper Canyon. That railway line is over 390 miles (650 km) in length, crosses 39 bridges (the longest bridge is over 500 meters long) and 86 tunnels (the longest over 1,500 meters).

We departed from El Fuerte, Sinaloa, (second stop from the Pacific side) where we had found comfortable seats in the last train-car, with plenty of window space and all luggage taken care of by porters. Points of interest were handed out on a sheet, but most of the time they were a bit exaggerated or over-rated in my opinion. Things like a small Indian grave-yard, or the longest bridge were either hard to spot or not that impressive. Once we left the plains, the scenery got more interesting and the number of tunnels and bridges became impressive with often great views over valleys or down deep into some canyons. Not the Copper Canyon however, that one we would not see for another few days. We climbed slowly but surely with a 5% grade into a Ponderosa Pine forest.

At one point we went for coffee and some sweets in the dining-car. About 20% of the light bulbs there were burned out, which made me realize the condition this so called first-class train actually was in. The coffee was lousy, and the cake was dry, stale and rather expensive. Half the seats in the train were empty this Wednesday, while it was 'high season.' Security was quite high however, with a few muscular guys in camouflage uniforms toting heavy automatic machine-guns around. Obviously, this is the state of Sinaloa, drug-lord country after all.

Around noon we got to a station at Cerocahui where we would get off the train and went by van over a very dusty road for about

10 km to the remote 'Paraiso de Oso Lodge.' A.s.k.a. 'Bear Lodge, a cool place at 5,400'. A quick lunch was served with a delicious *'zucchini sopa'* and filled jalapeño peppers and orange-cake for desert. That afternoon we were on our first hike in the pine-countryside. It had been a long time for us since we had seen trees like that as we had left Canada five months earlier.

There are still cacti at this elevation. Beaver cactus, which has much wider leaves than the regular Nopal or Prickly Pear. Arizona Medrona (Arbutus) Southern Oak and Chihuahua Pine were all new species for me while on our way to a large cave with remnants from 50 terminally ill Indians who died here in the 1920ies.

Back at the lodge, it turned cold as soon as the sun went down, but fortunately we had a wood burning stove in the room. A small bag with petrol-drenched sawdust lit the wood in no time.

The next day we left the lodge for the small town of Cerocahui to visit the late 18th century mission and hotel of the same name. Very picturesque and there was a special mountain ambiance to the hotel. The trip continued with kitchen staff following us to a fabulous lookout point over the magnificent Ulrique and Copper Canyons. A warm, three-course lunch was catered here on this very impressive spot which we could fully enjoy while the meal was prepared. After an hour we took the rough road with uncountable hair-pins down to the small village of Ulrique. This town is not worth all the hassle of getting there, it's rather plain and it lacks older houses and the Indians are long gone. But the views on the way down were fabulous with an abundant bird-life. Along the river, down below it was hot, 32 Celsius, while on top it is cool, with a complete different flora and fauna.

The next day, we had all the time in the world because the train we needed to catch was not leaving until 1 pm. Lunch-boxes were supplied which we devoured while waiting in the dusty station because food was not allowed on the train (unless purchased on board). The ride was only a few hours, but the scenery was stunning with so many tunnels. In one we turned around 180 degrees without noticing anything of it unfortunately. Higher and higher, we could see our next hotel long in advance. Called the Castle at Areponapuchi, it was more like an outdated mansion from the fifties in a rather bizarre style. The dining room was nice with large chandeliers and a huge fireplace, but the cottages were Spartan to say the least and with noisy gas heaters.

A short but steep walk brought us to the rim of the canyon with splendid views. From down below we could hear the slow but constant drum from a few Tarahumara Indians going from house to house as is custom here during the 40 days of Lent. Right below the rim was a small Raramuri Indian settlement which we visited on the following morning's walk. At the settlement near the cave we bought some more straw and pine baskets. Some were laying half-finished in the large water-basin for being worked on. Cute kids were hanging around doors and dogs everywhere. Up to the Rim-side hotel, we bought a woven yellow shawl for about 90 pesos from one of the local women. Things like that would cost triple in Todos Santos. By 11 o'clock it started to rain and shortly after some thunder struck the area and a real downpour set in.

Lunch, which we had at the hotel, was not bad, but by now the rain changed into wet snow which was not so nice. At the train station we first didn't dare to get out of the van until signs of the approaching train were eminent. Inside the decrepit waiting room for the *Chihuahua El Pacifico* train, a lot of dust was stirred up from kicking a half deflated basketball around to keep us warm. At one point, the ball kicked up high, disappeared through one of the missing windows just as a whistle in the distance announced the arrival of the train. Location, about 8,000' high, in the small village of Areponapuchi, we were on the third leg of the adventure through the Copper Canyon in Mexico.

Driving through clouds and heavy rain made this short section to Creel not the best part. A stop at Diversadero could have made for a nice photo session, but I got off without my camera. The spectacle there, amplified by the torrential rain, was the real Mexico craziness that I had expected all along whenever the train would pull into a town or village. Crazy things happened here. The minute I jumped off the train, (the drop was over two feet) as there is no station platform, the train's whistle goes off and the huge mass of steel starts moving again. Backwards, thanks God, disappearing nearly out of sight. At the same time, it is raining cats and dogs. Trying to find shelter, I squeezed with lots of other people under the few umbrellas and tin roofs we could find. Despite the rain, this place is an orgy for the senses that should have lasted longer. One-man food-stalls prepare the most exotic ingredients on fires in old oil drums. Another whistle sounds; the west-bound train is arriving. More peasants and tourists arrive at the little food-stalls. Yelling kids rush by, a bonanza for pickpockets. Giggling Indian girls, some in traditional dress, others in too tight blue-jeans cross the street. A police with a small whistle in his mouth tries to keep order in the chaos of traffic. I walk down from the station, as only a short distance from this spectacle, there is another. One of the best lookouts at the Copper- Tararecua- and Ulrique canyons- three in one.

Back to the train, it was impossible to ignore the colorful Indian women with their arms full with woven baskets. Strangely enough, their prices were fixed; saved me the bartering and not to miss my train. On one of the side tracks, there was a long line of flat-bed cars with gigantic motor homes tied down on them. Since the area is impossible for this sort of vehicles, people travel in their motor home on the train; having organized dinners and showers at certain hotels along the way.

During the next part, the train crosses the continental divide a few times and if that's not enough excitement, an engineer's delight called 'El Lazo' where the tracks go under and then over itself within the length of one mile is next. Around 3 pm. We got to Creel where we disembarked with wet snow coming down on us. Is this Mexico?

The following day, our trip to the bottom of the canyon took about six hours and was nothing less than phenomenal. With a few stops at breathtaking lookouts, we got lucky while the day progressed, the weather turned nice again and once we were down in Batopilas, it was warm and the hotel, just before the town, overlooking the river turned out to be a gem. It wasn't old, but had the charm of an old Hacienda. The room had character; the food was great and the people, Arturo and Veronica, very nice. We got laundry done and with dinner, I made sure I had first pick at the rather limited selection of wine. The second night, the choice in wine was really slim, but OK. under the circumstances. After we toured the quaint little town of Batopilas, we went by car to the lost Church of Satevo. Only eight km out, but more than half an hour to get at because of the road condition. We had to bribe *Jose*, the local guide, to get us there because he claimed it was not on the itinerary. The road was not only winding and rough, but so narrow at spots that the driver had to back up at times to let upcoming traffic go by. It was worth the trip, mind you. This mission-church from the late 1700s stands there very pristine, all by itself and in reasonable good shape.

Back in Batopilas, we looked for a suitable lunch place. One of them was booked solid by a group we saw quite a few times this trip, the birders. We had birders in our group, someone called them 'twitchers' (not twitters) a common British expression indicating their nervousness when it comes to the exciting moment of adding one more species on their life-list. Thanks to them, because I would not have spotted them, we saw red-tailed and black hawks. They were flying awesomely alongside us for some time during our decent yesterday into the canyon.

Today, we went up and up, almost 6000 feet to get out of the canyon and all under sunny skies. Some Tarahumara Indians were walking along the side of the road and across the valley along the 'Camino Real' in their typical 'diaper'-like loin-cloths. It's a very colorful dress and I had trouble imagining that there are 60,000 of them out here living in the mountains. They are excellent long-distance runners but not competitive, reason I guess we never hear or see them at Marathons or Olympics.

In the capital of the state Chihuahua we tried to do a tour on a trolley that was advertised to run daily in the morning. But this is Mexico, despite being assured at the tourist office that the trolley would run today, there was no evidence of it. Instead we took a local bus for 3 pesos each and got off near the Pancho Villa estate. This place is now an interesting museum and was open today. Peaceful now, but Pancho's original car, a 1919 Dodge, full of bullet holes from his assassination, was a stark reminder of different times.

0--0-0-0-

Practice makes Perfect.
(About friends of us that stayed at an all-inclusive)

After a lapse of several years, Frank and Charlene, a semi-retired stock broker and his trophy wife stepped off the plane in San Jose. It was a gorgeous afternoon, maybe a bit on the warm side for a couple that just escaped the long dark winter north of the 49th parallel. Not that they lived in igloos up there as most Americans believe, but a change for warmer climes can be nice once in a while. They were looking forward to making peaceful use of their time-share they were talked into when they were in Cabo and had a few drinks too many a few years ago.

Frank is still puzzled about that purchase. He does not even like hot climates because he cannot show off his favorite tie and jacket and refuses to wear shorts. The sun will do more damage than good to his pale skin and balding head he thinks, making him a good candidate for a large sombrero. But Frank would rather spend his money on brand-name designer clothes and shoes. His lovely wife on the other hand, adores the sun and she could not wait to get her tight little butt on a lounge-chair next to a pristine pool.

Once through customs, Frank found out that there isn't much choice in taxis as they have set rates and are all controlled by the same company. A giant Mexican chauffeur ushered them to a big SUV which they needed for their oversize luggage. In the car, Charlene pushed the windows down and let the wind ruffle her long blond hair during the speedy ride along the toll road to the hotel strip.

Since their time-share purchase they have used their week at many other places and when they arrived at the hotel, they didn't recognize the place.

A huge, iridescent green banner screamed 'Welcome to sales team USA.' The once pastoral setting was now cluttered with many more hotels all around. They also noticed that the hotel was not really kept up too well despite their yearly increasing maintenance fees and to make things worse, the place was booked that week for a national Gatorade sales convention. A 4-story high blow-up juice bottle and a massive alligator were swaying in the wind while loud blaring music was echoing through the corridors when they checked in.

Frank however, likes quiet times, reading, and playing classical music for which he had brought a few instruments which explains the bulky luggage. At home he practices his music almost obsessively, one hour, early, every morning before he goes to his brokerage office in town. When they booked their stay, he had specifically requested a corner room so only neighbors on one side would have to keep up with his practice. Frank obviously didn't remember that the walls were more like cardboard, so that did not work out too well.

After one morning of ardent trying to master some complicated passages in Paganini's cello concerto, the front desk called about the neighbors in room 213. They had complained that someone might have a cat in the room which makes horrible sounds at an unacceptable time in the morning. The next day Frank practiced later in the morning, so the busy sounds of cleaning crew, room-service, traffic and overhead air-planes would cover his attempts to attack Paganini again. This was not only nicer for the neighbors in 213 but suited his wife much better also, as by that time, the pool would be open, and she could install herself close to the bar instead of suffering the early morning practice in the room with supper-sized earplugs in her cute little ears.

On one of his walks a few days later, Frank explored the beach and found a beautiful spot behind a rock formation, out of the way from the hotel rooms and he decided to play there one of his other instruments, the flute, next morning at sunrise.

Armed with a flashlight and one of his favorite silver flutes, Frank has a whole collection of them, a music stand, sheet music of some popular classics and a ball-cap as it was still a bit chilly, Frank sneaked out of the room and went to the beach. Once set up behind the rocks, he got so inspired that he played piece after piece without interruptions or mistakes. After the sun came up higher in the sky, he started to perspire and put his ball-cap upside down on the ground in front of him. By now, several joggers were running along the beach and one of them stopped to listen for a while. Frank was totally not used to perform for strangers, he got nervous and missed a note or two. The jogger felt sorry for him and dropped a twenty-peso bill in the hat of a by now flabbergasted stockbroker. Then, as the jogger went on his way again, the jogger said, "Keep on playing senor, practice makes perfect."

"OK" said Frank, "and you keep running, keeps you in shape!"

-0-0-0-0-

The mysterious cave paintings in Baja

Ever since driving through Baja, it has been my intention to take at one point some extra time to visit the ancient cave paintings in the Sierra de la Francisco north of San Ignacio. As this is about the halfway point between Tijuana and Cabo, it always has been a favorite pit-stop, but we always rush through. On the way south, too eager to reach the warm waters of the Sea of Cortez, and going north; well no good excuse actually other than to go home and see my sons after months of playtime down in paradise.

One year on my trip back I was not in a hurry and took the time to make the arrangements to line up a guide to hike to the caves. On the day I arrived in San Ignacio, one of the finest small towns in Baja, I checked out the variety of tours offered by the different offices that surround the small central plaza. Around the corner is an exposition on the caves and the government office where you have to register and pay the fees. They also set you up with a local guide who is radioed about your arrival the next day.

As the caves are far off the main highway and one is not allowed in without a guide, it is best to go with a tour of which there are basically two offered. Both take about 6 to 8 hours. One is to the easier accessible *'pinturas rupestres'* at *'Cueva Ratôn'* near the small village of San Francisco de la Sierra. The other, the one I preferred is harder to get at but offers two caves in a wonderful setting about a two-hour hike into the mountains from the village of Santa Martha. This site is called El Palmarito I and II. The prices are about the same with all the tour companies, but they require a minimum number to make it workable. As I was all by myself, it became rather pricey, so I opted to find my own driver. Somehow, I ran into Manuel Pilar Arce, the owner of a campground and eco tour company 'Los Petates.' He took my tourist visa and 282 pesos to the registry office and set it up for the next morning. 200 pesos were going to the local guide, 37 pesos for entry the sites and 45 pesos gave me a permit to make pictures or video. Altogether a lot of tickets, forms and stamps as is custom for any government transaction in Mexico. All I had to work out still was the taxi to Santa Martha and back, each about two hours driving.

At 6 am Manuel picked me up with his van and raced along Hwy 1 east in the pitch dark. After 45 minutes he suddenly took a left down on a gravel road where he still kept up a speed of about 40 mph. Soon the sun was piercing over the *Tres Virgenes*, the volcanic mountain chain further east. We were going north into the mountains through river beds and cactus forests for over an hour before we reached the ecological reserve of Santa Martha. Here is where we picked up Eduardo, my local mountain guide for the hike to the caves.

When I signed in at the village, a look through the book showed how few people come to this site. None the day before and three *Americanos* the day before that. I checked my backpack for water, some food and found myself a good walking stick. At the early hour and some overcast in the sky the two of us went up the trail without much difficulty. It is just the last kilometer that turns almost into a scramble directly uphill, but then you are almost in view of this magical place which seemed to draw me nearer and nearer.

Eduardo proved to be not much of a talker and if he did it was strictly Spanish. We happened to be of the same age resulting in an easy equal pace. Once we were about 200 yards below the cave, we reached a fence with a small gate for which Eduardo had a key. When I looked up, I was in awe, seeing the huge murals under the overhanging cliff stretching out before me. With the stillness only broken by the tunes of some songbirds, I tried to take it all in. I almost forgot to take out my camera, but once I did, I could not stop shooting.

The Palmita cave site is actually a huge cliff overhang, about 150 feet long by 40' high and almost 50' deep at its most inward curve. This one and many others in the area were known for centuries by missionaries, Indians and early travelers. In prehistoric time and during the mission periods folks must have traveled in close range to this site. The huge mural has several layers of paintings above one and other. How they reached that high is all part of the mystery and why some human figures wear headdresses is also not fully understood. From the animal pictures it is quite clear that the early inhabitants of the Baja peninsula were hunters. Two large deer facing each other look like they are ready to fight. A black mountain lion is also noticeable in the paintings. Most men-figures wear so called 'sak-hats' and there is one woman with a similar headdress. Strangely enough, most human figures are dressed; at least the pictures give the impression of red shirts and black pants. However, when the first Jesuits came here from Spain they found to their embarrassment, the natives running around completely naked. Was there a higher civilization before them? It all depends on how you interpret the paintings.

After 30 minutes we went on to the second cave which was just a short walk along a narrow ridge infested with goat droppings. Right then I heard the lonesome bells from a few goats down below. This much smaller site has an interesting painting of about a dozen hares in a row. The folks that painted here were obviously aware of whales as one painting depicts clearly a *balena*.

The mysterious Baja Cave paintings are absolutely fascinating because of their age, the primitive forms and designs and last but not least; their beautiful, warm, earthy colors.

My visit to the cave paintings was an awesome experience, something I can highly recommend for anyone with an interest in the past and who likes to hike deep into the desert with the safety of a guide.

-0-0-0-0-

Ever seen a Green-flash?

During many happy hours I have been looking to that distant Westerly horizon. It made me think of that elusive phenomenon 'the Green Flash'. When you research it, it doesn't seem so elusive. There is a good explanation for the green flash, which I will come to in a minute. The problem I have with it is that I have hardly ever seen a green flash while I have tried so often since I can see the western horizon from my casita. When we have guests, we often take them to the roof top patio. Is it their imagination or am I blind? Five out of ten, my guests see the flash and I don't. Perhaps I have always been too generous with serving our drinks.

Green flashes are real, not illusory phenomena that can be seen at sunrise and sunset. With the help of Dr. T.A. Clark, Professor, Department of Physics, University of Calgary, I came to the following explanation. Since the beaches around Todos Santos are mostly facing west, we have a good chance to catch the flash. Sunset is often around one of the many happy hours' we gringos adhere to giving us even more chance to watch this intriguing phenomenon. Now since that time of day, not all of us might always be completely sober, it is sometimes difficult to distinguish between an illusion and the real thing.

The word 'flash' refers to the sudden appearance and brief duration of this green color, which usually lasts for only a second or two at our latitude. As the sun nears the horizon it appears to be flattened out. To have the right conditions, there should be no obstruction between you and the setting sun, not a cloud in front of the sun.

The reason the sun gets redder as it begins to set, is that the light must travel farther through the atmosphere before it gets to your eye. The shorter wavelengths of light, especially blues, are scattered in the atmosphere. Only the longer wavelengths, red and oranges, are left in the direct beam that reaches our eyes. The lower the sun the greater is this effect. The narrow band of green at the top of the sun just before it does dip below the horizon is the shorter wavelength that is not fully scattered off.

This green flash effect is only present near sunset and only visible to the naked eye when atmospheric conditions are right, and the sun has dipped below the horizon. Before I did my research on this subject I did not know that the same thing happens in reversed order at sun rise. So, to the early risers on the East Cape, I suggest trying this out for themselves. I came across a report of a successful sunrise green flash that was once reported in 1983 by Paul Doherty in the United States. He wrote "I was standing on Table Rock in the Linville Gorge Wilderness of North Carolina. It was just before dawn. I studied the eastern horizon and managed to spot a green flash at sunrise! Wow! Then the sun rose as a red ball including a rare naked eye sunspot! What a morning. The drive from Michigan had been well worth it."

Did you ever experience a blue flash? Oh yes, some would say, plenty of times, usually after a few too many. Now serious, the blue light from the sun can under extreme conditions cause a 'blue flash.' Normally the atmosphere scatters the blue light to the side more than green and the red light, so that the blue is removed and there is no blue flash. However, rarely, the atmosphere will be so clear that the blue light will not be scattered as much, and this can lead to a very rare blue flash. This should not be confused with the much more common effect experienced during or after an exorbitant night of quaffing out on the town.

Cheers and *hasta luego*.

-0-0-0-0-

Food and Drinks

National Nacho Day

There is this trend of celebrating special food days, like a pizza day, donuts day, or taco day. You name it, and there is a day claimed on the calendar for a certain food, either spontaneously invented by an influential foodie or by marketing from a particular company. So there is a particular food for every day of the year. October 4, 2016 was National Taco Day and November 6 is ordained to 'National Nacho Day.' This of course, fits perfectly in the ex-pat's lifestyle as they try to have a good time anywhere in Mexico and have easy access to good nachos.

Now what is considered a good nacho, varies of course from person to person. Originally nachos were rather simple, small tortillas with cheese and salsa. Nowadays we throw a lot more stuff on there, so they can replace a whole meal. Wikipedia describes nachos as a popular food based on nixtamalized corn, of Mexican origin that can be either made quickly to serve as a snack or prepared with more ingredients to make a full meal. This nixtamalized word can be a bit of a tongue-crusher but is no joke and comes from nixtamalization. This is a process that entails the preparation of maize, corn or other grain, in which the product is soaked and cooked in an alkaline solution, usually lime-water, and then hulled or husked from its protective outer layer. In their simplest form, nachos are tortilla chips covered in melted or shredded cheese, salsa and sliced jalapeño.

Nachos originated in the city of Piedras Negras, Coahuila, around 1943, at a restaurant called the Victory Club. This town is just over the border from Eagle Pass, Texas, and home to a military base. What happened, and this is apparently a true story, the wives of several US soldiers from nearby Eagle Pass were in Piedras Negras on a shopping trip and arrived at the restaurant after it had just closed for the day. The ladies must have begged chef Ignacio Anaya to make them something, so Ignacio, called 'Nacho,' threw a dish together for them with what little he had available in the kitchen: tortillas and cheese. He cut the tortillas into triangles and fried them, then added yellow Wisconsin cheese and called the dish Nachos Especiales, or Nacho's Specialty. From there, the popularity of the "nacho" spread throughout Texas and the word "nachos" appeared in an English dictionary for the first time in 1949. It took however, another 20 years before the nacho became popular outside of Texas. In the 70's, the popular sports journalist Howard Cosell was given a plate of nachos during a taping of Monday Night Football, and liked them so much, he kept talking about them for weeks, which introduced the nacho to a whole new audience.

Later, Ignacio went on to work at 'The Moderno Restaurant', in Piedras Negras, and eventually opened up his own Nacho restaurant in the same town. And now until this day, both places still use the original recipe. You don't have to be in Mexico to find an interesting variation, from the simple or plain nacho to the piled up, like a mountain high plate of nachos with ingredients from here to Acapulco; this is something you can try anywhere or anytime. But on November 6, it is worth celebrating 'national nacho day' in a restaurant or at home. With the right company and enough *cervezas*, you can have a sweet party that will carry you over until bigger events will take place later in the month.

-0-0-0-0-

Talking about Mangoes
from a talk on the phone with my Mexican house-sitter

"Wow, your mango tree looks good this year," Agustin said.

"Yes," I said, "you must have many new mangoes."

"Yeah, that will be lots of mango juice for me," said Agustin (because I will not be there when they are ripe).

"Mangoes to peel and eat. Mango paste, mango pasta, you name it," Agustin rubbed in.

"You know," I said, "It will take two to mango, and I am not there."

"Oh, but I have lots of friends. A mango here, a mango there, mangos everywhere," he said.

"We'll eat succulent Mangoes until we die."

Mangoes are delicious in smoothies, luscious in salsa but can be a slimy, slippery challenge to cut. The best way to go about it is to start first with a ripe, but still firm fruit. If the mango is too ripe, it will be a mushy mess, and hard to cut into pieces, though easy enough to scoop out for pulp.

Late summer when they are ripe, the town has a Mango Fiesta. Food and music are hugely intertwined at most fiestas.

Now this is how you attack a mango. Look at the mango and realize it has a flattish oblong pit in the center of it. Your objective is to cut along the sides of the pit, separating the flesh from the pit. Holding the mango with one hand, stand it on its end, stem side down. Standing the mango up like this you should be able to imagine the alignment of the flat, oval pit inside. With a sharp knife in your other hand, cut from the top of the mango, down one side of the pit. Then repeat with the other side. You should end up with three pieces - two halves, and a middle section that includes the pit.

Next, take a mango half and use a knife to make length- and crosswise cuts in it, but try not to cut through the peel. At this point you may be able to peel the segments right off the peel with your fingers. Or, you can use a small paring knife to cut away the pieces from the peel.

Last, take the mango piece with the pit, lay it flat on the cutting board. Use a paring knife to cut out the pit and remove the peel.

-0-0-0-0-

Mexican Beer

It is hard to imagine any fiesta in Mexico without *cerveza*. Beer has become the most popular drink to celebrate anything in Mexico. Even on non-fiesta days, beer consumption has reached huge proportions per capita. Several factors have played a role in beer's popularity. History for one and low taxation in the 1900's to keep the cost down so peasants would switch from the rather damaging habits of drinking *Pulque* (pronounced pool-kay) to *cerveza*. Then came a wide availability of beers and of course, an insatiable thirst in a hot and dusty country that has made beer the most popular drink in Mexico.

Before the existence of beer, the Aztecs and Mayas made their own fermented concoctions from grain or corn. Later on, *Pulque* and *Mescal* were popular, but these drinks had devastating effects on people. Its production was unsanitary while its sale was mostly in filthy squalid bars.

The thousands of people that made the annual pilgrimages to the god of drunkenness, Ome Tochtli in Tepoxtlaá, often arrived grubby and sodden, goofy from over consumption of cheap pulque. When German immigrants and the influence of a brief 'Habsburg' rule over Mexico in the middle of the 19th century happened, modern-day beer brewing became an all-Mexican endeavor.

The Austrian Emperor Maximilian ruled Mexico for only four years but had a lasting effect on the future of beer consumption in Mexico. This chap never traveled without his brew-masters. As a result, two brands of Mexican beer, Negra Modelo and Dos Equis Ámber, are like the darker, more malty subset of German lagers known as 'Vienna style'. While not as heavy as most British ales, the Mexican 'Viennas' are fuller bodied with more malty sweetness and character than pale pilsners.

The first commercial lager beer brewery in Mexico was La Pila Seca, founded in 1845 by a Swiss immigrant. Soon there was the opening of the Cervecería Toluca y México, by another Swiss brewer and in 1869 Cerveceria Cruz Blanca was founded in Mexico City. While at first, most breweries were small operations, by 1890, the first substantial industrial brewing facility in Mexico was built in Monterrey for Cervecería Cuauhtémoc.

Prohibition in the United States boosted the Mexican brewing industry in the 1920ies as Americans flocked to border cities to purchase and went crazy on alcohol. Several new breweries opened on the Mexican side of the border in places such as Tecate and Mexicali.

Today, most Mexican beers are produced by the two beer giants, FEMSA and Grupo Modelo. FEMSA which is now owned by the Dutch brewery Heineken, has about 44% market share and is a general beverage corporation whose roots date back to 1890 and that first large Mexican brewery in Monterrey. With their brands; Tecate, Sol, Dos Equis, Carta Blanca, Superior, Indio, Bohemia and Noche Buena – FEMSA is a major international brewery. Grupo Modelo, the competition of FEMSA, has fewer brands but is actually larger with more than half of the market share due in part of its export. They make the famous Corona, Corona Light, Negra Modelo, Modelo Especial, Modelo Light, and Pacífico and Victoria.

The Mexican market is the world's eighth-largest by volume and

Corona is the most popular Mexican brew outside of Mexico. The strange thing is however, that some Mexican brands are hard to come by in some parts of Mexico. Carta Blanca for one, while it is such a great beer. One beer critique describes it as *"The best Mexican beer I've ever had, and easily one of the best lagers overall. It compliments Mexican food so well, it's unbelievable. It has a nice flavor, high in alcohol, no hint of being watered down. This makes Corona look like tap water"*.

Talking about water; did you know that for every liter of beer most breweries need about six to eight liters of water? For that, it is interesting to read a recent statement made by Anheuser-Busch, the world's number one beer maker headquartered in Brussels Belgium. In light of a 'Better World' commitment, it is trying to reduce water consumption during the brewing process. They targeted to use only 3.5 hecto-liters of water for each hecto-liter of beer by the end of 2012. That's a huge reduction, fine as long as the quality of the beer does not suffer because of it. One thing I noticed since Heineken has taken over FEMSA; my favorite Dos Equis Amber is now finally for sale in Baja.

Thanks Ome Tochtli.

-0-0-0-0-

Microbreweries in Mexico

In the last few years, microbreweries are trying to find a niche (like everywhere else) in Mexico which proves to be very difficult as only two companies hold nearly 100 percent of the domestic market. Even though Mexico is known worldwide for its beer, those two companies determine what millions of people swig. Where one brand is on tap the competition cannot. Mexican craft brewers in the *"Por la Cerveza Libre"* movement hope to change that. The two large conglomerates, each own dozens of subsidiary distributors, bottlers and malt producers. Competitors have long accused the companies of engaging in monopolistic practices.

In 2006, the federal government's competition watchdog found Grupo Modelo had engaged in antitrust activity by entering into exclusive rights agreements with sites selling its bottled beers. The company successfully appealed the decision.

Despite all that, the craft brewery movement in Mexico has been growing for only a few years now, inspired by microbreweries in the United States and Canada. But in that short time, Mexican brewers have launched one of Latin America's largest beer-tasting festivals in the country's second biggest city, Guadalajara. They opened a series of bars under the name El Deposito there as well as in Mexico City and Puerto Vallarta that double as stores to sell their creations. The *"Por la Cerveza* Libre" movement was hatched in 2014 in one such El Deposito bar in a swank Mexico City neighborhood.

The bar is designed to look like a clandestine liquor depot during the Prohibition era in the United States and is decorated with pictures of Al Capone and other gangsters of the period. The centerpiece is a piece of equipment made to look like an old distillery. El Deposito's exposed-brick walls could come straight out of Portland, Oregon, except for the Mexican twist in the brews: One alcohol-rich barley-wine by Cerveceria Cucapa is aged in tequila barrels. And Cerveceria Minerva's Malverde, an American-style pilsner, is named for Jesus Malverde, "patron saint" to the country's drug traffickers.

Mexican craft brewing is now at the point their U.S. counterparts were in the early 1980s: basically zero. The country's microbreweries, numbering now just over a dozen, account for less than 1 percent of Mexico's beer market.

Cheers!

National Margarita Day

February 22 is one of those completely made up and unnecessary holidays that you can't help but love because it makes for a valid excuse to throw a party. Who was the smart-ass that came up with the idea to call February 22 National Margarita Day is just as mysterious as who invented the margarita. The fact is that next to tequila and Corona, the margarita is the epitome of Mexican drinks that has become incredibly popular on both sides of the border. With National Margarita Day you are invited to try new recipes and get together with friends to toast on this delightful cocktail.

As for the origin of the margarita, it is like the many stories about who invented the pizza. Many places claim to have invented the margarita, but nobody really knows. For that reason, the stories about the inception of the margarita cocktail are as numerous as the variations on its recipe. Some accounts are quite vague, others are farfetched. I am not chauvinistic, but the most likable story claims the origin to be right here in Baja California. The northern part of Baja that is, in a bar at the Riviera del Pacifico

Hotel and Casino in Ensenada to be exact. In 1938 Danny Herrera, a renowned Mexican bartender at the casino was completely in love with Marjorie King, an American actress who hated taking tequila pure while tequila was also the only liquor that her body could tolerate. Finicky girl as she was, Herrera used his ingenuity to impress her and mixed the best ingredients to meet Marjorie's predicament. A third of tequila, a third Triple Sec and a third of fresh lime juice made Marjorie, who was called Margarita in Mexico, utterly happy. The word spread around and soon enough the 'Margarita' became one of the world's most famous cocktails.

Another tale that traces the origin of the margarita back to Baja sounds more believable then the previous one. Enrique Bastate Gutierrez from Tijuana claims to have created the Margarita as homage to actress Rita Hayworth, whose real name was Margarita Cansino. As a teenager, Margarita Cansino worked as a dancer at the Foreign Club, in Tijuana, where she inspired the bartender's creativity which resulted in this famous cocktail. This was obviously before Hayworth adopted her screen name, which dates the origin of the margarita back to mid-1930.

There are many more stories about the invention of the margarita and some of them can be found in 'The Great Margarita Book', a 146-page colorful and informative creation by Al Lucero with a foreword by Robert Redford. The latter is obviously an extreme margarita connoisseur while Lucero has been mixing and serving margaritas for over 20 years at the bar in the famous Maria's Restaurant in Santa Fe, New Mexico. The second edition has 90 recipes of tasty margaritas that are basically prepared the same way but with the emphasis on different ingredients. The descriptions in variation of tequilas from ordinary *reposado* to premium and super-premium can be a true eye opener.

National Margarita Day challenges us to try different recipes which can give you real insight about the subtle differences between tequila. A good margarita, crushed, on ice or straight up never tastes better than on a sunny patio around a pool or on the beach. For everyday happy hour I keep mine simple, but perhaps for this special occasion I might try a premium tequila in my margarita. A simple recipe is as follows; two parts of reasonable tequila, one part of Controy and one part of fresh squeezed lime with some course sea-salt to balance it off. If you want to tone it down a notch or keep your weight under control, try a Margarita Light. This concoction saves calories as well as your mental and physical abilities. Take 1 1/2 oz. tequila, 2 oz. diet lemon-lime soda, 3 oz. diet lemonade, a splash of lime juice on 1 cup of Ice. For a dazzling array of other Margarita recipes, there is a book '101 Margaritas by Kim Haasarud. Around 10 dollars at Amazon. https://is.gd/o8DAHH

This is an amazing compilation of margarita recipes with one for every colour coordinated occasion and events throughout the year.

-0-0-0-0-

If Mescal would be a guy, Tequila could be his sister

Not that tequila is for sissies, but mescal, which seems to gain huge popularity lately, is with its earthy and smoky taste definitely a guys drink while tequila is often enjoyed by both genders. Not long ago, in Mexico's back country it was often difficult to find tequila. Instead all they had was bootlegged hooch and the firm belief that it would raise a man's soul to its true height.

Mescal was the catchall term for these spirits distilled from different varieties of the agave plant and usually sold in recycled plastic soda bottles. Therefor mescal has always been looked upon as a cheap alternative to tequila. But that has changed as some producers have found methods to refine their product and set up ways to export their mescal to trendy bars and restaurants in the southern US and Canada.

Mescal is produced from the maguey plant (member of the Agave family) and was one of the most sacred plants in pre-Hispanic Mexico as it was used in religious rituals.

Unlike tequila, which comes from the blue agave and a restricted area, the maguey plant can be found all over Mexico but the production for mescal is mainly in the state of Oaxaca. According to Wikipedia there are 330,000 hectares cultivated for mescal and owned by about 9,000 producers. They make over six million liters annually with more than 150 brand names.

The origin of mescal is not certain, but there is a myth, as there are about so many things in Mexico. It is said that a lightning bolt struck an agave plant that instantly cooked the inside and opened it, releasing its juice. For this reason, the liquid is called the "elixir of the gods." Before the Spaniards invaded the new World, Aztecs were able to distill a drink called Pulque. Apparently, the Spaniards didn't like that too much and as their stock of European brandy ran out, (they learned distillation from the Moors some 700 years earlier) they started to experiment with local plants.

Now there is a long tradition of handcrafting mescal on a small-scale. A village in the state of Oaxaca can contain several production houses, called *palenques*, each using methods that have been passed down from generation to generation. Some of them are using the same techniques from 200 years ago. The process begins by harvesting the plants. This is a heavy job as the spiky leaves must be sheared from the maguey, making them look like huge mutant pineapples. The heart or piña can take the size of a laundry basket and can weigh 80 to 170 pounds each. Once they have enough, the *piñas* are cooked for about three days in underground pit ovens. This roasting in earthen mounds over pits of hot rocks gives mescal its intense and distinctive smoky flavor. Once that process is finished the *piñas* are crushed and mashed traditionally by a Flinstonian wheel, called a tahona which is pulled and turned by a mule or a donkey. The mash is then left to ferment in large vats or barrels with added water. At this point it only makes for a beverage with the strength of beer or wine which calls for distillation to make it stronger.

Just like with tequila, there is even a secondary distillation involved making it a strong 78-80 proof (38-40% alcohol) drink. Depending on the duration and the containers the end product is kept in, you get like with tequila, the general classifications such as plain blanco, *reposado* (two months old) or *añejo* (over a year on oak). There are a lot of varieties in mescal due to added spices, flavors added and differences in processes, like chicken can be added in the tank during distillation making for a typical taste besides the smokiness. Then there is 'gusano' or gusanito, the mescal with the famous worm in the bottle.

Mescal is seldom used in cocktails but consumed pure and preferably with Oaxaca cheese or *chapulines* (fried grasshoppers) on the side. There is a well know saying about drinking mescal: *"para todo mal, mescal, y para todo bien*

también" translating into "for everything bad, there is mescal; for everything good there is the same."

And as for its popularity outside of Mexico, the US and Japan buy most of the 25 million dollars' worth of export. At Poblano Escobar, a popular bar in LA., they have moved away from the traditional pure mescal and developed a cocktail called Mayan sacrifice and 400 Rabbits. According to a patron, *"this cocktail has just enough balance of spiciness and smokiness to bring tears to your eyes"*. Other bars in LA. with an interesting mescal selection are Las Perlas and El Diablo. I was just in Vancouver Canada, where at La Mescaleria, an upstage bar/restaurant had a special on: 4 meat tacos, 1 Pacifico and a shot of tequila or mescal for $18. So, this way, even far outside Mexico one can support the 29,000 people that are apparently working in the mescal production.

Salud!

-0-0-0-0-

Is Mexican wine any good?

There is actually a pretty extensive history about wine in Mexico. Not much has been documented and expectations have not been very high until recently. The first grapes, Vitis Vinifer, were brought to the Americas, North and South, from Europe and were planted in Mexico by the Spanish in the early 1500s.

This was long before they arrived in any other part of the New World. After unsuccessful attempts by Spanish conquistadors to grow wine grapes in the tropical areas of Mexico, cuttings were planted alongside the native varietals which grew abundantly in Parras Valley in the State of Coahuila. Soon after grapes were introduced to other regions such as Puebla and Zacatecas.

Nobody knows for sure what the initial grape varietal was that first crossed the Atlantic, but what we know is the grape was referred to as the common black grape of Spain, and that it gave rise to the mission grape of California, the Criolla Grande.

The planting of vinifera grapes was ordered by Hernan Cortes around 1520 after the supply he had brought dwindled. During the next century and a half wine production in Mexico skyrocketed.

Casa Madero, the first commercial winery, was established by Lorenze Garcia in Santa Maria de las Parras (Coahuila) in 1597 and is still in operation today, making it not only the oldest Mexican winery, but the oldest in the entire Americas.

Over time, the demand for Spanish wine imports dropped off which resulted in a ban in 1699 on wine production in the country save for church requirements. This ban was not officially lifted until Mexico's independence.

The ban of course, did not stop the Mexican wine producers entirely. Juan Ugarte, a Jesuit priest, was one of the many who continued making wine despite the ban. He introduced the first vines to Baja California upon his relocation to Loreto in 1701. From there the vines were transported to Santo Tomas Mission south of Ensenada. Things moved slowly in those days, so it took the Jesuits to 1791 to establish the Santo Tomas Mission. And then it took another half century before they worked the exceptional fine soil conditions in the Guadalupe Valley, a short distance north of Ensenada. By that time, in 1843, it was the thirsty Dominicans who started wine production at the Mission Nuestra Senora de Guadelupe del Norte.

During the next 50 years, the era of wars had a pretty negative effect on wine making in Mexico. The vineyard's land was seized by the state and redistributed. However, in 1888 the Santo Tomas Mission was revived as a commercial winery by private investors and now operates as Bodegas Santo Tomas. From that period until 1910 wine-making spread once again. A group of Russian immigrants (the Molokans) fled the Czar's army in Europe and relocated to the Guadalupe Valley and surrounding areas. There they began making good quality wines, only to be stifled by the Mexican Revolution.

Much later, in the 1980s there has been a small revival again especially in the Guadalupe Valley. Foreign competition and a general lack of good grape varieties and agricultural knowledge made it still a struggle. Over time and with imported skills and experience from France and Italy, some small wineries have sprung up since the 90s. Now they have started to produce some excellent wines that can match any product from the Napa Valley.

In August every year, the Guadalupe Valley in Northern Baja hosts *Fiesta de la Vendimia,* a grandiose wine and food tasting event spread over several weeks while the grapes in the area are ripening for the next harvest. *Vendimia* means 'harvest of wine-grapes' which will be soon following the fiesta. At times there can be more than half a dozen events going on simultaneously on one day. From actual crushing of grapes and live music performances to Tango shows and candlelight dinners.

Mexican Wine, part Two

The previous chapter introduced you to the history and how the production of wine came to Baja California. This second part focuses on what is now actually produced in northern Baja.

Despite the general opinion that traveling Northern Baja is dangerous and irresponsible, I dodged the bullets and dared to visit nearly a dozen wineries recently. What a nice surprise that was! The so called *'Ruta del Vino'* is nowadays well marked with rustic wooden signs along the route pointing to more then 20 wineries where tasting can be arranged by appointment or by simply walk-in.

The most known valley for wine production in northern Baja is the Guadalupe Valley which is just one of seven valleys that are dedicated to the cultivation of grapes between Ensenada and Tecate. The valleys together produce 90% of all Mexican wines, or 1.3 million cases of wine a year, of which 25% is exported abroad. In a matter of 25 years, from when there were only a few wineries, the region has expanded east and south and there are now nearly 70 different vineyards.

Most people think Mexico is too hot for growing wine that has elegance and finesse, but that is not true. According to Robert Whitley, a San Diego-based wine columnist who has been keeping tabs on the Guadalupe Valley for almost 30 years, said: *"It's probably cooler than Napa Valley in summertime. But you have that diurnal effect of grapes having sunshine and warmth during the day that they need to ripen, and the cooling at night that preserves the freshness and the acidity. So it's actually an ideal climate for grape growing".*

Only a 15 minutes' drive from where Highway 3 leaves the coastal toll-route north of Ensenada, you enter Mexico's prime wine region. One of the larger wineries that is easily accessible and open for tasting most days of the week is *Viña de Liceaga*. Besides a rather sweet Rosareo, I tasted a full-bodied red called Sofia from 2010. But their 43/60 Reserva was the best with 50% Cabernet, 25 % Merlot and 25% Syrah (Shiraz). Their tasting room is a good start as they open early.
A little further east on Highway 3, I drove up into the narrow country side roads to find *Viñas de Garza* and *Tres Mujeres*. This last one is a much more laid-back operation by three women with a very small production. The reds were a bit on the heavy side but her presentation in the underground cave-like setting was rather out of the ordinary.
To get to the village of El Povenir, which is the center of the valley, the best way is to drive to the town of Francisco Zarco where you

turn left by the Pemex station. El Povenir has a small but fascinating *Museo del Vino*. At the corner of one of the side streets I visited J.C.Bravo, a mid-size boutique winery where I bought a few bottles of Palomino, a refreshing white, medium dry from 2011. Palomino is one of the original Spanish grape varieties and since I was going to Spain shortly after, I liked to get a taste of it.

I passed Monte Xanic and Chateau Camu which are both up in the hills and off the highway a bit but worth a visit if you can call ahead. (646-174-6155 for Xanic and 646-171-9300 for Camu) They produce over 40,000 and 15,000 cases of fine wines respectively.

Further along the highway towards Tecate, there are the two large producers, Pedro Domec and L.A. Cetto. You can't miss them and their tasting rooms are open every day from 9.30 to 3.30. Domec produces a lot of grapes mostly for ordinary table wines and as base for their El Presidente Brandy. However, LA Cetto now cultivates 2,500 acres of vineyards and produces over one million cases of wine which count for more than half of Mexico's wine. Besides quality Cabernet Sauvignon they produce a very fine Nebbiolo, a soft and round tasting red specialty wine. Theirs is considered the best in North America, on par with those from Italy's Piedmont region, and it has even been listed on menus in Parisian wine bars.

There is a third large producer, but most of their acres are south of Ensenada in the Santo Tomas Valley and on towards San Vincente. This is Bodegas de Santo Tomas and is actually Baja's oldest winery. They were established in 1888 but grapes were already grown in the region by the Dominicans in 1791 at their Mission of Santo Tomas. After restructuring, planting better grape varieties and building a top notch crushing and fermentation facility south of Ensenada, their wines are getting better all the time.

The winery I personally enjoyed the most however was back, just west of El Povenir and called Bibayoff. This winery was established by a Russian Molokan family that arrived in Baja around 1906 and got their official production permit in the 1930's. In their eclectic tasting room, I found the grandson of the pioneers, David Bibayoff now himself a grandpa, behind the bar pouring generous size tastings of white red and rosé. It was the atmosphere and the intriguing origin and originality in the labels and their wine names that was most likable. A blend of zinfandel and colombard, not the most elegant wines, were bottled and called Rosayoff and tasted quite palatable. Their 2009 zinfandel was a rich and round tasting wine from which I brought a few bottles back home. David knows how to entertain his guests in the utmost laid back tasting room in the Guadalupe Valley.

Now if Baja wines are so good, why don't you see more of them on supermarket shelves in the States you might wonder. Explanations range from high import tariffs, to the fact that most of these wineries simply don't produce enough to meet even domestic demand, let alone international. So, while in Mexico, surprise yourself or your guests and look for a local wine next time you shop.

-0-0-0-0-

The not so Fun Part

The 'Mordida

This is the common term for 'bribe,' which feels apparently like 'a bite' as the word really means in Spanish. Another term in our language is 'kick-back' and it is not always clear who gets kicked or bitten. I am sure you have heard horror stories about the Federal police bribing folks using the road in Mexico. Over the 12 years we have been driving in Mexico, and often for five or six months a year, we got bribed only three times.

When it happens, it comes as a shock to you, so it is absolutely not fun. You should not go along with it, if you can avoid it. Meaning, play dumb or use another language then Spanish or English to confuse them unless there is ground for holding you up because you made a clear traffic violation.

Once we got away with that, but the first time it happened, it did not. It was early morning, little traffic in Tijuana and we had bikes on top of the car, too easy to spot. This guy on a motorbike flagged us down, and I doubted that he even was a real policeman. I asked ID and he showed me something that did not convince me entirely. He asked for 100 dollars. I asked him for what?

"You were speeding over 80 in a 50 zone."

I was certain that I had not, and we argued back and forth for some time. He was not letting go and insisted to get us to the Tijuana police station. Well that must scare even the most hardened people, because that is the last place you ever want to end up. So that worked for him, but as we just arrived over the border, we had no pesos in the equivalent amount and while driving through the states we basically use plastic, so we had no dollars either. We told him that we had some Canadian money and reluctantly, he would accept that. We got my wife's wallet and cleaned it out entirely for which he provided a used brown envelope. He was looking around him before he dropped the envelope through my side window and all we could find was 32 Canadian and some change. I put it in the dirty envelope and handed it back to him. Without looking in to it, he took off and so did we, rather shocked from this early morning encounter.

The other two times were in La Paz, southern Baja. Again, minimal infractions. Both ignoring a stop sign, which most locals do but your foreign license-plate is quickly noticed and taken advantage of. It also depends on what time of year. This was close to Christmas with an obviously strong need for cash to buy the kids presents.

Again, it felt bad, and it made for one extra reason to decide importing our little car and put Mexican plates on it so we would not be such an easy target any more.

-0--0-0-0-

Night of the Cucaracha

When we took possession of our hacienda, the place was thoroughly cleaned, and most pests were fumigated more or less, '*mas o menos*,' being the keywords here. Because, for three enduring nights we had a conundrum in the bedroom. Every time my wife got into the room, which was on the second floor and had to be accessed by an outdoor staircase, a large, fat cockroach was waiting for her on the night-table. As soon as the light was turned on, the despicable sucker scuttled away and was nowhere to be found. Visions came back to me from a night in a rented casita a year earlier (see Casita Azul). It was a large studio with a huge hand-tied palapa roof that came with all the droppings of dust, bugs and what not. I was trying to get asleep in the charming Spanish-ironwork bed when after a while I heard something dropping down every so often, about twelve seconds apart, to be exact. Having caught several roaches earlier that evening, all I could think of was, more of those creepy critters.

My nerves took hold of me and all I could do was count the elapsed time between each drop, just as you count the seconds between lightning when a severe thunderstorm hits you and you want to know if it's getting closer or drifting away.

At that frequency, I imagined, a cockroach tumbling down from the thatched roof into the sink every twelve seconds, ergo five per minute. That would be 300 in the next hour if I didn't do anything about this. We would be swamped and buried under thousands of creepy crawlers by daybreak.

I got from the bed, found my torchlight next to my slippers on the floor and made my way to the galley area. A look in the sink found nothing. There being two, I check the other sink. Again, no trace of any black conspicuous crawler. Completely befuddled, I shine my light up to the slanted roof, nothing there either. Was it all imagination? No, there it was again, 'blob,' right next to me, from the counter where the large blue potable water bottle stands. A growing wet spot below it on the concrete floor made it all clear. It was only a leaking tap and I got off easy this time.

But not tonight. Knowing you have a cucaracha in the bedroom and saying, "Have a nice sleep", sounds great but does not work under the circumstances. When the roach was gone, we couldn't find him anywhere and after a lengthy search through the large bed- and bathroom, my wife and I end up exhausted in bed and couldn't sleep. We knew he was out there and every time, just before one of us would doze off into nirvana, you think you feel the creepy bugger crawling over your face and we were wide-awake.

Tonight, I was going to make an end to this nightmarish

occurrence and I am happy to quote one of the few things I still remember from my early Latin classes, Julius Caesar's "Veni, Vidi Vici." Before my wife would go up, I went upstairs, armed with a can of Raid and a miner's lamp on my head. I went into the room under the light of a waxing moon that shone through the French doors. I closed the door carefully behind me and shuffled quietly on my sandals over the glazed tile floor to my wife's bedside. With my left hand I turned on the light on my head, keeping the Raid ready in the other. There he was, sitting somewhat frozen only for a second or two, again on the wooden night table. Whoa! That's him, snooping on some spilled wine or so I thought, and gave him a good dose from the spray-can. Despite all the carefully planned effort he still got away, but not far. One more squirt and he was scampering less quickly, perhaps from the wine or the Raid, but coming in my direction again.

"Wrong way, guy," and 'smack' went my sandal. Size 11 came in handy and made the cucaracha history. 'I came, looked and triumphed.' I felt like a hero, but still don't completely understand why these creatures are so detested. Isn't it a bit discriminating? Yes, they do look disgusting, but so do a lot of other insects but they don't get the same paranoid reaction from spouses or daughters in-law. Once a roach is sighted they scream and yell as if it is the end of the world. Anyway, we slept happily ever after, at least that night. How long before we'll have another cucaracha in the bedroom, time will tell.

-0-0-0-0-

The negative side of paid help around the house.

Once you get a cleaning lady or gardener on a regular basis, they become your employees. That would be fine as long as it works out. But try to eliminate or fire someone is a difficult matter in Mexico as the following experience will show.

When we took possession of our house, the gardener came with it. Noe was an enthusiastic and hardworking fellow who announced himself always whistling traditional Mexican songs when he entered the property. But a guy with the collective skills and great attitude could do better than work 6 hours at 40 pesos an hour, of course. So we lost him despite giving him a nice Christmas bonus. The New Year left us searching for a new gardener and finding one that had a morning open in his schedule.

The new gardener was quite the opposite from Noe, who was such a joy to have around.

The following story shows how this turned out a few years later.

The hunt for Chuy

He was recommended to us by a retired Mexican lady we knew, who lived in our *bario* where Chuy takes care of her garden once a week. He is quite an introverted fellow, short, but very strong and has few friends. Thursday is his day there, so I tried to catch him as he had not shown up for many weeks at our place and would have liked to let him go.

The lady told me he didn't show this week at her place either because of *Semana Santa*. Nothing goes according to plan during the week before Easter. I told her the amount of money we offered Chuy as a settlement just to get rid of him. She shook her head and could not believe he didn't take it. We wanted to solve this problem before we go back north I told her and asked her to give me a call when Chuy showed up.

"OK," she promised.

A year earlier, it came to a point that we had enough of Chuy's poor performance. Often not showing up and when he did, it could be any day of the week or drunk on a Sunday morning, but never on days Ejido water was running through the canal which he should have used to water our plants. That, he refused to do period. So we tried to get rid of him. However, in Mexico it is very difficult and costly to fire someone. The alternative is to make them miserable, so they quit. Someone suggested letting some snakes loose in the garden, rattlers preferably, that will put him on the run. Others suggested we cut his wage in half or just tell him you're broke. Somehow Chuy found out we were unhappy with him and suddenly he came regular and worked a little harder. So he hung on for another year, but now he had not showed up for the last three months.

Then one day, Chuy was at our gate with an official, a lawyer as it turned out, who didn't speak any English. Out of a confusing Spanglish conversation it became clear; Chuy wants money because he thinks he is laid-off since Christmas. He had picked up his Christmas bonus but never came to work since.

The lady that recommended Chuy acted as mediator for a while and we agreed to have him work on *Martes*, the day *Ejido* water is running in the canal. He promised to come to work again but never showed. First the excuse was no transportation then his mother was sick, and now it is April.

Mexican law is nasty about firing somebody so our stand was, that he quit (one who does not show up for work three times in a row without contact or reason is considered to have quit). However, this was for us to prove. Not a simple matter with the language barrier. We agreed to talk again the next day when Chuy and his lawyer would come with a translator.

An hour later, on our way to 'La Esquina' for happy hour, a large sedan followed us with Chuy, his lawyer and Castro, a guy in his late twenties who speaks good English. We stopped and start a conversation at a street corner where after some time finally the amount Chuy wants comes out; 30,000 pesos (2,500 US) Good Lord! Even his lawyer thinks that's a bit high. Castro looked totally embarrassed; that a Mexican tries to screw a gringo over for so much money while he has offered the guy work. I asked what it adds up to if you take all the social costs, vacation etc. for a severance pay.

"Twenty percent," his lawyer said. I started calculating on the back of a grocery bill by lack of anything better and figured out that for the four years he worked, this would add up to 8,800 pesos and that is what we offered him.

"Be reasonable" Castro tells Chuy with no avail. Now Chuy says he quits and would take it to arbitration obviously upon recommendation of his layer who smells a cut.

As we parted, I told them that we were soon leaving for Canada, and that he should take our offer. No, Chuy stuck to arbitration which made us worried. After some more time arguing back and forth and telling him that it will be November before we can respond to arbitration. We shook hands on the offer and agreed to have papers and the money ready the next day. We set up a time for the meeting and drove into town to pick up the money from an ATM.

The following day, neither Chuy nor his lawyer show. Around 5.30 I called Castro. The first time I met him I was a bit afraid of him as he has a creepy scarred face, a greasy navy cut, is stocky, muscular and wears only black. But he turned out to be a nice guy and became very helpful. He knew where Chuy lived and suggested that he go over there to find out about the deal and call me back.

Thirty minutes later he was on the phone; Chuy wasn't home, but via a friend of his he got to talk to him.

"Not good news," he says. "Chuy has changed his mind."
Now what! That shithead of a lawyer of course has a hand in this. That night I had a horrible sleep, dreaming about court in La Paz with lawyers and translators and bills from here to Jericho. It became a nightmare, waking me up all sweaty and miserable.
The next day I prepared a *'Finiquito'* form with the settlement on it and I tried to figure out how to get it to Chuy. At 4.30 I called Castro who had offered to help, because he sees that this Chuy guy is pure *'loco'* as he calls it. He happened to get off work in 15 minutes. I invited him over for a few beers and we had a good talk. He learned his English in California and Washington during a 10-year stint north of the border. He was an illegal immigrant and jumped the border somewhere in the Sonora desert by crossing the river with a bunch of other guys. He had seen several dead bodies on the way but kept going and found work but eventually ended up in jail for an invalid driver's license and was deported back to Mexico. In the meantime, he had 3 kids and a wife in the US, a wife and kid here in Todos and lives now with his father in an old RV that a friendly gringo left them.

We decided to go to town with a bundle of cash in my pocket and two copies of the form and look for Chuy. We climbed into my little car and I follow Castro's instructions to Chuy's home. This is in San Vincente, one of the poorest neighborhoods in Todos Santos. Dusty dirt roads with lots of garbage along the sides, chickens running loose, many cats and barking dogs surround the place. The house is actually more like a small sand-stone hut in the corner of a dirt lot with some rusty old cars that seem to have been sitting on blocks for eternity. A grubby elderly man came out which was apparently Chuy's father. Castro walked towards him to find out if Chuy is home. Nada, he is supposed to be at his brother's, two blocks up the street. We drove on and at the next place I followed Castro into what people here call 'home.' The front room was windowless, and plaster had fallen off the walls and ceiling making the inside look like a war scene. A few bare light bulbs dangle from the ceiling and I heard a lot of voices in the back of the house. After a while Castro came to the front and shook his head.

"Well, we tried," I said, and drove Castro to his house to drop him off and he introduced me to his father who runs the town's funeral service.

Between a huge collection of broken toys, household appliances and old cars sit a large black, almost antique funeral hearse. Obviously there has not been a recent death in town because the hearse is very dusty and has a flat tire. On the lot is the old RV looking like it will never move again.

Castro's father, Ricardo came out and gave me a pleasant firm handshake. He is much better looking than his son and wears an Alaska red-checkered flannel logger's shirt and conversed in good English. He said he knew Chuy better than his son, and he will talk to him, to try make him see the light. I left the papers with him and told him that if he gets them signed, there is 500 pesos in it for repairs on his son's car. "OK," he said, "I will talk to Chuy later this evening, when he is drunk, that might help."

I drove home a little bit more relaxed. Nothing really accomplished, but somehow it felt better with the support from these friendly strangers. Or are they also taking me to the cleaners, I wondered? They could put a fake signature on the papers and take the money. As this was going through my mind I was also curious to know if Chuy went for arbitration or not. Now it was almost Easter weekend, government offices will be closed until Monday.

On Friday morning after breakfast I called Ricardo and found out that he spoke to Chuy last night and that he was not going to budge. But he said, "I will walk over again and talk to him this morning." We agreed that I would come by around noon before I would go away for the weekend.

When I got to Ricardo's place, there were three women doing laundry and some cooking in the open and I asked if Ricardo was around. He came out of a little shed and told me that he had spoken to Chuy twice now without result. I made a comment about the three women around and asked him which one was his.

"My wife passed away some years ago" he said with a sorry voice.

"They are my sister in law and her daughters."

"I am sorry to hear that, but they seem to take good care of you."

"Yes, they come by once a week."

Then I asked him if he would give it another try over the weekend and I walked back to my car to go camping for the weekend.

On Easter Monday nothing happened. No phone call from Ricardo or Castro.

By Wednesday I called the lady where Chuy still worked to remind her about her promise. The next morning, she calls that he is working her garden until about eleven. I look for the stash of money, print off a fresh *Finequito* form, and I hurried over to catch Chuy.

At the gate, he walked up to me and wanted to shake hands. He was rather friendly but wanted the lady to read the papers for him. Trouble was, she did not want to get involved anymore then she already was and refused come out of her house. Next, I showed Chuy 17 bills of 500 pesos, all spread out like a deck of cards. He is licking his lips but is not going to take it. I tell him once more we are leaving tomorrow for La Paz and back to Canada.

"When are you back," he asked in Spanish.

"Not until late November. You better take the money now," I tried once more. But he was not going to bite. He said he will come by this afternoon with someone to talk.

"With your lawyer?" I asked.

"You will see," he said.

I left very frustrated and felt defeated because I knew he would never show. Better let it go now, I thought. We'll see when we get served or there will be a lien put on our property.

Against all odds, at 4 o'clock that afternoon, Chuy showed up at our gate with another fellow. Same age or maybe even younger then Chuy, not his lawyer. Salvador is his name and speaks no English, but his facial expression was friendly and likable. So what was he doing here? Apparently Chuy wants the money and Salvador was here to read the *Finequito* contract. He read it out loud for Chuy to hear, because as I now realize, Chuy cannot read. I should have cued in earlier, but how often do you meet an illiterate person in your life. Finally, he put his full name at the bottom of the paper and signed. Salvador witnessed the handling and the deal was done. Chuy was almost in tears when he counted the bills and said we are 'amigos' again. I was not so sure about that!

-0-0-0-0-

Horror story – Scared Campers

In the winter of 2003, while talking to a few campers as they were packing it in on this gorgeous white sandy beach overlooking Danzante Island, we asked them why they left.

"Out of water and beer," they replied. But when we probed a little bit further, they explained, "Now with only three campers left, we question our safety here at this remote beach. Particularly after stories we heard about a couple from Kelowna that was ambushed, robbed blind, their car stolen, and the dog shot dead." Apparently, this horror story was now circulating for two weeks and was confirmed by friends of us in Canada. They had read the same thing in the paper. It happened far north in the Baja, where they were camping on a secluded beach somewhere near Rosario, between Ensenada and Tijuana. Traumatized and with serious injuries, one had been flown back to Canada while the other was still in a Mexican hospital. This can happen, obviously, and often the Mexican media try to keep a lid on it to keep the tourists coming.

-0-0-0-0-

Six fires in one day. Arsonists caught but go out free

One day a few years ago, the Todos Santos *Bomberos* (firefighters) had to put out six fires in one evening, all started by the same five people aged between 15 and 27. The pyromaniacs were caught in a little green Toyota Celica, containing a gasoline can, empty beer bottles and old rags; the recipe for Molotov cocktails. They set the fires at random and appeared to be students, three female and two male, admitted to the crime and were held one night at the police station but let go the following day.

Mexicans and gringos alike were steaming about this mode of action by their public servants and demanded answers from them. On Monday morning March 28, 2011 a 'Town Forum' was set up by Oscar Rosales, himself a victim of an earlier fire in February. He had five civic leaders invited to face the angry public of *Peublo Magico*. About 150 people attended, one third Mexicans, the balance gringos.

The delegate of the *Ministerio Publico* was the first to take the stand and explained what to do when you are a victim of any crime. The proper procedures were not followed by the victims in this case. The police putting with that, the blame of letting the arsonists go free on the victims. Of the six fire victims, only one came forward and happened to be family of one or two of the arsonists. They worked out a settlement for the claim about that fire between themselves removing the so called *'denuncia'* or accusation, which resulted that the arsonists being let go. Free of all the other damages because the others did not follow the proper procedures.

One *gringo* who was also a victim and identified the arsonists at the station, spend over three hours there talking about what happened and about her damages with no other result then to see the arsonists being let go. You can talk for hours to the police, but they don't give you the proper form or help the victim to fill it out.

The law states however, that after an offense, one can be held up to 72 hours in prison with no *denuncia.* The true answer as why they were let go was never answered. Is arson not considered a serious crime in Mexico?

Some Mexican women held emotional speeches in defense of the arsonists. A teacher who knew them from a young age on, expressed how very puzzled she was about their behavior and tried to put the blame on not enough psychological support in the community. This was also agreed upon by most other authorities and that there is not enough manpower in the police force and that there is no secretary even to take your report. It sounded like it is all La Paz's (the State's capital) fault, what they tried to say, except for the chief of *Bomberos*, *Senor Chava*, who was the only one who got a huge applause. He and his volunteers did a fantastic job that Wednesday night and in the weeks prior to that.

The Todos Santos *Bomberos* were under tremendous pressure. Their equipment was worn out or just not there. At the fire I witnessed, half the firefighters had no helmets while large beams overhead, fiercely on fire, could crash down on them anytime. At that same location was a large propane tank that nobody apparently had seen. The next day I saw how black it was and realized that things could have been a lot worse if that tank had exploded.

At this same 'Town Forum' the local Palapa Society who always funds the *Bomberos,* held a collection with the goal to reach $5,000 US to repair and keep the fire truck and ambulance on the road. 27,250 pesos were collected on the spot to keep the firetruck going.

-0-0-0-0-

Casita Azul

The casita sure was blue, cute, with an outside shower and a large open space with a palapa roof, hidden between huge bamboo and fruit trees. We moved in just in time to enjoy happy hour on the patio while the soft evening sun spread a beautiful light through the palm trees.

At night however, we got a different feeling about the place. Cold as it became, tiny geckos came alive and were running all over the adobe walls and ceilings, everywhere. My wife panicked.

"I am going to die! If one falls off the ceiling into my bed!" she yelled.

A moment later I saw a seven-centimeter-long, black creature crawling on the kitchen counter. I was not sure if cockroaches came that large and was not going to look it up in a reference book, so I crushed the sucker with the bottom of a wine bottle real fast. It gave me the creeps, and suddenly we were not that happy couple on a Mexican vacation any more. All night I heard sounds like mice crawling in or along the palapa roof. Every five minutes I heard something fall down near the kitchen counter. I went up to investigate with a flashlight thinking, if this were more of those roaches, with the frequencies of 12 per hour, there would be sixty or seventy of them crawling around tomorrow morning. I could not shake the idea, what a disaster it would be to try to kill them all. However, wherever I looked, I could not find anything. I waited in the cold to hear the sound, but of course nothing happened when you look for it. I went back to bed and turned the flashlight off but kept it really close.

Another night now, we had an enormous windstorm. No problems inside other than the noise, but the next morning we see thousands of little black pins, like small seeds, on the patio. While having breakfast out there, one of those exceptional mornings here in Todos Santos this time, I see one of the seeds move. There was no wind.

Soon I saw a few more moving. I swear, I had no rum in my coffee. The little pins were changing from tiny round seeds to oblong, moving objects in a matter of minutes. I still had trouble defining what they really were, but my wife was not going to wait for that. She took the broom and got rid of it real fast. A few were left here and there and as it turned out, they walked away as little ants an hour or so later. The wind on the patio must have blown all the larvae out of the palapa during the night. We could have come back a day later with thousands of ants over the house. How do people deal with this I wondered, if you leave a house unattended for some weeks or months? I guess you can be in for quite a surprise if you come back after six months.

-0-0-0-0-

Curious or what?

Not so horrifying as the previous story, but when we were renting a casita for a month right on the *Malecón*, I noticed something strange happening each night. Tonight, I finally came to write it down as I have been noticing the phenomenon for some time now, but could not believe it until I confirmed it.

Every evening around six O'clock a police car comes by and stops at our corner. A guy jumps out, opens, and closes an electrical box on the wall and leaves in a hurry. He goes so quickly, and nothing happens, as it appears. What was he doing?

Tonight, I went to the box to investigate. It just sits there open and is not protected, so I open it and see a switch and a lot of wires, some bare and exposed. I realized that it must be the light switch for the lights on the boulevard. Neon light, that takes some time as nothing happens for maybe ten minutes. Once they are heated up, they start to glow. That's why I could not link the police car and the boulevard lights. However, the scary part is, that the box with exposed wires is accessible to anyone. Even a kid could put their hands in it. Imagine what could happen? Should I have turned them off? Maybe it would have reduced the number of noisy visitors on the *Malecón* at night.

-0-0-0-0-

Canadian's hotel in Mexico seized by men with machetes ... and it was legal

From the Globe and Mail, August 26, 2016. Reported by Mike Hagar.

Graham Alexander was at a morning business meeting when his phone started buzzing with frantic calls and text messages from the staff at his hotel nearby, who said scores of armed men had arrived and were evicting everyone.

Mr. Alexander raced back to his 24-room hotel, in the Mexican resort town of Tulum, on the east coast of the Yucatan peninsula. He found the entrance padlocked, his guests out on the street and the furniture being tossed away. Two burly men told him to leave "or we'll take care of you," he said.

It was the morning of June 17. More than two months later, the Canadian businessman is still fighting to get back his hotel, despite concerns for his safety and puzzlement that the men he holds responsible for his misfortune may be in Canada.

What happened to Mr. Alexander, a former Vancouver Canada resident, was not unique. According to Mexican media reports, he was among more than a dozen hoteliers and other hospitality entrepreneurs who were evicted that morning in an ugly land dispute.

This is a cautionary tale about doing business in Tulum, or anywhere in Mexico for that matter. Tulum, south-west of Cancun, was once a sleepy village on the Riviera Maya that has grown into a tourist hot spot with boutique hotels, fashion shops and too many yoga classes. (author)

The June 17 evictions were only the latest episode in an ongoing feud over who owns the land accessing the palm trees and white sand of Tulum's beaches. Those supporting the eviction say it was a move to return the properties to people who actually *held* title to that land. But the hotel operators say they were muscled out of prime locations by rivals from another Mexican state. Mr. Alexander paid the municipality of Tulum his local taxes for this fiscal year, according to an injunction application he recently filed in a Cancun district.

Most of the land in Tulum was once part of an Ejido, communal farm land, but Mr. Alexander said he bought a lot that had been legally converted to private property more than a decade ago. * His injunction application states he has official copies proving he owns the property. He has had his human rights violated and lost his assets, all without a trial, the application alleges. The court docket identifies four members of a business family from Monterrey, the four brothers Schiavon, as the people who have challenged him for ownership of the land.

"I feel completely robbed. I put up way over $1-million to build this hotel. We put all this effort over so many years, believing we were the owners," Mr. Alexander said. "And these guys come in and do it as they did. If it was a legitimate operation, they would have never sent guys with machetes." Because he has dual Canadian-Mexican citizenship, Mr. Alexander is not bound by local law, which limits foreign ownership of land.
Around 2014, he received a warning from a neighbour, Roberto Palazuelos, a fellow hotel owner who is also known in Mexico as a television actor. Mr. Palazuelos told the Canadian that businessmen in Monterrey, a city 1,400 kilometers north, had a claim on the land. The actor suggested that Mr. Alexander try to make a financial settlement with the Schiavons.

Mr. Palazuelos said he agreed to pay the Schiavon brothers, and got a good deal, $250 per square meter for land that is now worth four times that sum. He said he then urged other hoteliers to settle with the Schiavons. "I tried to help as many people as I could," he said. The morning of June 17, Mr. Palazuelos's hotel was one of five that were spared. "Thank God my hotel was not *in that eviction," he wrote that day to his 97,000 Twitter followers.*

Renaud Jacquet, whose beachfront rental villa, Behla Tulum, was among the targeted properties, said about 300 men in black T-shirts marked with the word "Security" arrived, armed with machetes and sticks. The men said they were acting on an eviction court order. However, Mr. Jacquet said, the court order mentioned a complaint about a female tenant who allegedly was leasing the land from the Schiavons and had defaulted on her rent. As a result, Mr. Jacquet and the hoteliers were not parties to the court hearing and weren't notified that they would be expelled. "It's a complete aberration," he said.

Mr. Alexander and the other evicted hotel owners have now turned to the courts to seek injunctions. Some went to Mexico City to lobby politicians. They are also hoping that the election in their state, Quintana Roo, where the Institutional Revolutionary Party (PRI) of the incumbent governor, Roberto Borge, was defeated, will be a turning point. They are hoping that his successor, Carlos Joaquin Gonzalez, who takes office next month, will not tolerate the mess in Tulum.

* See important warnings in a later chapter called 'Different Properties.' In the Important section # 4.

Hurricanes

Coastal areas on either side of Mexico, are prone to hurricanes from May until October. Often weather reports and government send out warnings ahead of time and people get some time to prepare. But if it is a monster, despite the preparations, you just hope and pray for the best.

Mid-September 2014, hurricane Odile was one of the most intense tropical cyclones to have ever hit the Baja California peninsula. The cyclone made landfall near Cabo San Lucas, as a category 4 cyclone, causing widespread damage.

Thankfully, I was not there because of what I have heard from my house-sitter and other people, it was a horrible experience to live through. The build-up before it hits, the panic of picking up last minute food and drink-water supplies, and wood for boarding up while the skies are darkening, the humidity is rising, and the air-pressure is dropping causing a unrelenting headache and anxiety. The full impact came around 11pm. The noise from the wind seemed to be like three airplanes coming over low, all at once but then lasting for five or six hours! There was not a place that was not damaged by water and wind. Communication was out for days. Electricity the same and roads turned into muddy rivers. Months later the evidence was still all over the entire southern Baja.

Over the years we have had several threatening hurricanes, but most of the time they veered off to the Sea of Cortez, puttered out over the Pacific or lost strength at landfall turning them into a heavy tropical rainstorm or *chubasco.*

Do your preparations. I had made years ago boards for the major windows and doors. Never needed them until Odile hit. And thanks to our diligent house-sitter Agustin, who put them up in time, our damage on the house was limited to one broken window. Around the house we had a collapsed carport and palapa, the broken fence and palm trees that were out of anybody's control during the hurricane.

Ever cut off from electricity?

Regular electricity is for one who has lived on solar for five years very nice and pretty easy to get used to. We always got by on our solar panels that were hooked up to eight deep-cycle batteries. I had to be careful when my wife was ironing, and I used the sander or the drill at the same time. Same thing if we had three or four days of overcast in a row, but when does that happen in southern Baja?

One day we had a real problem. A few days before Christmas one year, when after some not so sunny days, I forgot to turn off the huge strings of outdoor Christmas lights at our driveway. We were not completely out of juice, but the system did shut off to protect the batteries from discharging below 20 percent. This is the amount set on most inverters to avoid damage to the batteries. That doesn't mean that there is no power left, but it made my wife rather panicky when the coffee maker didn't turn on that morning. I turned everything off in the house and we waited for the sun to come out, which brought our power back again.

The incident however made us aware of how vulnerable we were and once CFE (the National electricity provider) came into our neighborhood with 24/7 juice on a wire, we decided to hook up. The application is not complicated. You fill out a small questionnaire and you must have proof of domicile, like a water bill in your name will suffice. The actual connection is more problematic if it is going to be a first time. You are responsible for setting up the meter in a small cement structure at the edge of your property. If you don't go underground, the piping has to go upwards to a certain height, so the wires can be connected from across the street if needed without hanging too low for traffic. Also, you are responsible for the connection from the meter-box down and to the house. In my case to the bodega, where I have the main panel, batteries and inverter, out of the way of the elements.

For the months we are back up north we have a house sitter. Last summer he also went away for some time and the electric bill that comes normally every other month, got lost somehow in the process. He insists he never saw a bill. It's possible that it blew away during one of those nasty summer storms. Anyway, the account did not get paid and CFE doesn't give you much slack. They cut you off pretty quick and by the time we came back in November, we were still on solar power only. That was not in our plan, so I went to the CFE office in town with the last paid bill to get reconnected again. To bring that bill was smart. It made it very easy to look up the account and all I had to do was to pay 450 pesos re-connection fee and the outstanding balance. The big question now was when the power would be back on again. I asked the girl at the office and she said "mañana."

"Yeah right," I said. "Everything here is mañana. Seriously?" She said again, "mañana." Oh well, I thought, we will find out and I left the office with rather low expectations. The next day we had to go to La Paz and when we came back that afternoon, I could not wait to find out. A small *milagro* had happened. Our power was back on. Who would expect such efficiency in Mexico? However, for next summer, I hope to avoid the whole fuss by pre-paying the account. Apparently, you can do that with CFE and also with your water bills. The amounts are not huge, and it will make life a lot simpler for us gringos. Cheers to CFE for outstanding service.

After years of traveling around Mexico, staying in hotels and renting places we decided to find our own place.
If you ever consider buying property in Mexico, the next part is of great importance to you.

Part 4, The Important Stuff

Is it Safe

What is safe anyway? There's crime and violence everywhere, including in Mexico, I'm not disputing that. To be clear, violence in Mexico is no joke. There have been over 47,000 drug-related murders alone in the past five years. And there are homicides — an estimated 22 per 100,000 in 2012 which is more than three times the US rate of 4.8 per 100,000, but they are almost entirely drug-related.

Americans appear more reluctant to travel to Mexico than Canadians and Brits (5.7 million Americans visited in 2011 versus 1.5 million Canadians. However, only a handful even witness a crime, let alone, become the victim of one.

In my opinion, Mexico is generally a safe country and a great place to visit, to live or retire. But anybody who says they have never felt unsafe here is either naive or inexperienced. I have heard and read enough horror stories that at times make you think twice. The media feed on bad news and governments put out warnings, travel notices that are very general and for that matter scare people off. One has to think smart and use common sense. Don't drive at night if you can avoid it. Don't walk alone late at night and avoid dark alleys and bad parts of town. Lock up your place and don't flash expensive jewelry or watches.

I must admit that the first few nights in our own new home, we locked all the windows and slept with a machete under the mattress. Soon we relaxed and left the windows open for that lovely refreshing breeze at night and to hear the sound of the waves of the Pacific. Then when something had happened, a home invasion nearby or a sexual assault on the beach, you wake up and become more diligent. But during our last stay, three months early in 2016, we always had the windows open, the sliding type for which you can block the size of the opening with a stick or bar. We do the same thing in Canada

Except for border areas and four of Mexico's 31 states (all in the North): Chihuahua, Coahuila, Durango and Tamaulipas). Mexico is no more unsafe than Canada and safer than most big cities in the US. Don't select Tijuana or Ciudad Juarez as your retirement place in Mexico. The latter, also a border town of 1.3 million saw 8 to 11 murders a day in 2010 (accounts differ depending which news channel you believe). Ciudad Juarez is unlikely to ever be a tourism hot spot, but things have been quietly improving there. By 2011, CNN reported, the homicide rate dropped by 45%, and the following years saw this trend continue.

If you compare the data available and statistics from other places, Mexico looks quite good particularly when you zero in on Mexico's most popular travel destinations. For example, murder rates for Cancun and Puerto Vallarta, with rates of 1.83 and 5.9 respectively, are much lower than touristy Orlando with its Disney World at 7.5 murders per 100,000 residents in a given year according to the FBI and a Stanford University report.

Reports like the Texas Department of Public Safety that advised one year against 'spring break' travel *anywhere* in Mexico is a gross generalization and over-reaction. Mexico is a country the size of the UK, France, Germany, Spain and Italy combined. There are only pockets here and there where you don't want your kids to go and keep in mind that popular destinations like the Bahamas, Belize and Jamaica have far higher homicide rates (36, 42 and 52 per 100,000 respectively).

A Canadian travel writer, Robin Roberts, reported a while back in The Vancouver Sun, about wary travelers. She said, "those travelers have a lot to lose who buy into the media hyperbole and avoid Mexico as a travel or retirement destination."

"I've been traveling to Mexico for decades," she continues, "hell,

I even got married here. Since 2010, I've spent half the year in Mexico. I've driven thousands of kilometers from north to south, east to west. Have I ever felt unsafe? No. I have, however, felt uneasy in my hometown of Vancouver, a city with many back alleys I wouldn't dream of walking after dark."

According to Roberts, a hangover is the biggest danger you face when vacationing in Mexico. Well that might be the case for vacationers, it would not be a good thing for extended living or retiring in Mexico. I would say; look at the facts, exercise caution, and don't let the media hype make your decision for you.
To put it all in perspective, you are still more likely to get struck by lightning than to be murdered in Mexico. And, I would like you to look beyond those raw numbers and make an intelligent decision. I just want to give you the facts and let you reason things out.

Do I need a passport to go to Mexico?

The simple answer is YES. If you are a U.S. Citizen, you need one to return back to the U.S. As of June 1, 2009, any U.S. person over the age of 16 is required to have a Passport, Passport Card or other acceptable form of documentation (such as an enhanced ID, SENTRI pass, NEXUS or FAST pass) to travel to Mexico. Anyone else who flies in will need a passport at check-in. If you drive to Mexico, you of course bring your driver's license (valid in Mexico) besides your passport.

Tourist permit

If you fly to Mexico, you will receive the document that you must fill out and has been paid for when you booked your flight. Anyone crossing the border by land will also need that form: the FMT, or Tourist Card. You will pay about 390 pesos for that permit at the border and it has the same duration for up to 180 days (if you fill it out correctly). You need to stop at the border as you cross into Mexico. Look for the INM/SAT *Aduanas* building (immigration and customs). At the INM office you fill out the paperwork for the FMT. Then you go to B*anjercito,* which is a local bank where you pay for the FMT. Once paid for, take your receipt back to INM to complete the process and get your FMT stamped by an immigration official. You can get those permits in advance when you are a member of 'Discover Baja', saving you the hassle of getting your tourist card at the border. For more information, go to:

http://www.discoverbaja.com/go/fmm-tourist-permits/

What am I allowed to take into Mexico?

When crossing by land, you are allowed to take your personal belongings and $75 worth of merchandise, duty free. How splendid is that? People over the age of 18 may bring three liters of liquor or beer and up to six liters of wine. Do not bring fire arms. What am I allowed to bring back to the U.S. from Mexico? Your personal belongings and $800 worth of purchased merchandise, duty free. If you are a California resident over the age of 21 and crossing the border by car or foot, you may only bring back 1 liter of alcohol. Non-California residents over the age of 21 may bring back up to 60 liters of alcohol.

Vehicle Permits for mainland Mexico border crossings.

When driving your own car into Mexico it makes all the difference where you want to go, because most of mainland Mexico requires a vehicle permit which cost about 48 USD plus a bond in the amount between US$200 and US$400, depending on the make, model and age of the vehicle. The term of that permit is like your FMT, tourist card, up to a maximum of 180 days. If you don't leave Mexico with that car within that time limit, you lose the bond.

This vehicle permit which is valid for six months, can be used for multiple entry. The big thing is that you pay that deposit which is between 200 and 400 USD.

Motor-home and boat permits are valid for up to 10 years.

Only the owner of the vehicle can obtain the vehicle permit, and should bring copies of

- Title and current registration of the vehicle
- your passport
- your driver's license
- Tourist card which you buy at the border and enough cash or Visa/MC.

You probably want your deposit back, and for that reason it is very important that you remember to return your vehicle permit to a Banjercito (the bank for 'everybody') at a border crossing before your permit expires when you are leaving Mexico. Of course, bring your vehicle, your permit and sticker with you for your refund.

Exceptions for a Vehicle Permit

The good news is that the Baja Peninsula and a large part of the State of Sonora are exceptions to the vehicle permit rule, meaning you can just drive your car across the border into those

States without paperwork, bond or permits. All you need is insurance as discussed above. In those three States, Baja California Norte, Sur and a part of Sonora you can use your car indefinitely as long as your vehicle has valid and current US or Canadian plates, and the plates/stickers are kept current during the vehicle's stay anywhere in those three Mexican States.

Mainland Mexico thus requires extra paperwork, a +/- US$ 48 permit and a bond, to make sure you don't sell or leave your car behind in Mexico. The theory of the bond is to guarantee you take your car out again to protect the local car sales.

For boats and RV's, things have changed, and a temporary import permit is now required. However, those are valid for 10 years.

Permanently importing your car and getting a Mexican license plate and local Mexican car insurance is a whole different story. I imported a small car into Mexico and now buy local insurance, so I don't have to do that paperwork for getting double paid car insurance back. So now we fly to Mexico and just pick up our car out of storage at the airport.

Sounds easy and straight forward? Not so, just read on what a nightmare that can turn out to be.

Keeping your License plate current

Of course, you don't have to import your car into Mexico, but if you stay longer and your license plate expires, you better get it updated. The Mexican police has a keen eye for expired plates. People do one of two things, take the car back to the State or province to get the current decal, or they buy South Dakota license plates that apparently are easy to obtain.

Once your driver's license expires, you want that also renewed from South Dakota. To put insurance on the car, you might need an address in that State. That would not be a bad idea, as South Dakota has a low sales tax and other benefits for residents.

To have your mail forwarded, to have a postbox, insurance and to obtain a license plate, the following link can take care of it all. www.mydakotaaddress.com This company provides all the services you need to establish a South Dakota residency in the tax friendly State.

Importing a car permanently into Mexico

First off, your car has to be made in a NAFTA country, which is OK for U.S. and Canada made cars. Second, the importation should be done right at the border. In my case that would have been Tijuana. That idea by itself gave me the creeps, as it can take up to a day and a half by official custom brokers. Tijuana is not a place you want to hang around for too long.

What we did, is drive through to Cabo on purchased 'out of country insurance' and asked around for options here. That resulted in a contact from a 'friend' of a friend's uncle or cousin, to a rather shady figure who knew a way around the system. First, they tell you, you have to drive the car back to the border. Over 1,000 miles and back, and be stuck in Tijuana, no thanks! I decided to meet the guy one evening and he told me to come up with 650 dollars and all the paperwork such as ownership, visa and what not. He would get the paperwork and money to Tijuana with a five-day turnaround. Sounded good, and we would meet again after he had confirmed some inquiries and would give me a call. Two days later, after dark, I got the call. "Meet me in town. Bring the money and all your papers." As I did not have all the cash yet, I asked him to meet at the ATM by the only bank in town. I was thinking; is this a set-up or can I trust this guy? He had told me he works at a car dealership in Cabo and if things would go wrong, I could find him there. I drove into town and met him and took some more information from him. Gave him the original owner's papers (kept some copies) and the stack of money, all in pesos.

When everything was done I should receive a new two page green Mexican 'title' and a *factura* - the tax document in Mexico - indicating the import fee is paid. A week later, nothing. Even two weeks later no sound from Castro as was his name. My wife and I went to the dealership in Cabo and yes, there he was behind the counter in the parts department. He got out for a moment and promised to speed things up. A week later he came to town and *'milagro,'* he had the importation in order.

This all happened in 2006. Things can change rather quickly in Mexico and below you can read an update on current conditions from an article placed on the Baja Insider website by James Glover, Nov.1st, 2015.

Importation of cars into Mexico requires now that the vehicle be not newer then 4 years and not older than 10. One can have different reason for importing the car. Ours was to leave the car behind as to avoid the long drive twice a year, now that flying is so much easier and faster. Also, with a Mexican plated car we feel less a target of local police or the *Federales* and avoid possibilities for bribing. But be aware what you aim for as the following story from the same source mentioned above warns you for driving Mexican plated cars.

Importing a vehicle by a foreigner (from the U.S. or Canada) has become more necessary with some of the immigration law changes here in Mexico. It is in fact according to Mexican Customs illegal for a permanent resident of Mexico to drive a foreign plated car. This has been debated by many people and

I've been told it is not true. However, if you ask the *Federales de Camino* or *Aduana* they will in fact tell you it is Mexico Federal law.

Since it is a Federal law many of the local police in different cities may tell you it is okay to drive a U.S. plated car as long as they hold a U.S. license. Yes, in fact as far as they are concerned it is legal, but it is not according to the Federal authorities and they are the ones that could confiscate your vehicle. It has already happened repeatedly at the Cabo airport and I spoke to the U.S. consulates office who explained that lawyers are trying to recover almost 50 vehicles at this time.

Steps for importing your car

For whatever reason you may want or need to import a vehicle these are the steps that you must make in order to properly import, register and insure your foreign vehicle from the United States or Canada.

First you must use a customs broker or freight forwarder at the border to complete these steps and be sure when you contact them that you receive an estimate of the total costs to do so, which will require you providing the VIN (Vehicle ID number) make, model and year of manufacture. Only NAFTA (Mexican, American and Canadian) built cars may be imported. The way to know whether your car is a NAFTA built car is to look at the VIN as it should begin with a number 1,2,3,4 or 5.

The costs to import should include all charges; the bulk of which is the 16% IVA (Sales tax) based on vehicle value and then the broker's fees and a few government fees. Confirm with the broker that this is the total costs with no extra charges later, so that you know exactly what they will want for payment and in many cases, cash is what they will require, so confirm the method of payment as well.

They will also let you know if there is any problem with importing your vehicle at this time. Not all vehicles can be imported into Mexico. Remember, your car must be at least 5 years old and not over 10 years old. Mr. Glover recommends using the ACV Import Company as he personally used them in October of 2013 and they handled it very professionally and quickly.

The next step is to have your vehicle cleared by U.S. customs if it is coming from the U.S. and this can take up to a week to complete. You may wait at the border while this step is being done or you may send your original title to the freight forwarder so that they can do this before you arrive with your car.

It is the American side that requires up to a week to be sure the car is not stolen and is prepared to be properly exported. With some of the recent changes in Mexico it seems to be taking longer to import than it used to. Ask whatever broker/forwarder you are planning on using as to how long they estimate the importation to take.

The next step after forwarding your title is to take everything out of your car. Leave nothing but the spare tire and jack. Everything else must be out of the car or the brokers and authorities will refuse to do the job. That means if you are traveling south and have a car full of stuff you will have to arrange to leave it in the U.S. till the car arrives on the Tijuana side and then you will have to cross back into the U.S. to pick up your goods. The car being empty is really for your protection: while it can be a hassle, no one wants to be responsible for your personal goods. You may also of course leave your goods on the Mexican side of the border and then cross back just to import the empty vehicle.

You should now prepare copies of your Mexican driver license or a Government issued Photo ID (Valid US License is accepted) which is required. When you leave your vehicle, the broker should photograph the entire car inside and out. This is for your protection so that you and the brokers are sure if there has been any damage done to your car while it is in their hands.

Leave a copy of your driver's license and make your payment and be sure to get a receipt or *factura* if needed and be sure to remove your U.S. or Canadian plates before you leave your car. Once notified you may go pick up your car on the Mexican side. The folks at ACV offered to deliver the car at the hotel and in most cases, they will help get your car to you if need be. Get a bid for your insurance before you import your car. Once you have your car imported you will need to fax or email copies of the *Hojas de Pedimiento de Importacion* (Green Sheets) to the insurance broker and your payment to activate your Mexican insurance.

The final import papers or *Pedimiento de Importacion* will either be green for *Fronterra* or White sheets for National plated vehicles. The majority of what you will pay is for the I.V.A. (Sales tax) and it will be based on the value of the import set by the customs agents many times using the U.S. "Blue Book" values. The *Fronterra* plates are only for Baja California and Baja California Sur and will be treated as foreign plates if you go to mainland Mexico. This means a bond is required just as if you had U.S. plates and therefore the National plates do have greater value at resale.

Once you have the car imported, you want to go to the area you live in Mexico to register it; not at the border unless you live there. To legally drive your vehicle without plates from the border, you should go to the *Transito* and obtain a temporary 30-day permit. If this is not easily feasible you may copy your *Hojas de Pedimiento* and put the first page in the back window for the police to see. Then you can drive the car south to your destination with no problems and then obtain a 30-day permit at your local *Tranisto* to give you time to get your new plates.

Since the Jan. 1, 2014 changes to *Aduana* (customs) and SAT rules, it is possible again for private individuals to import your car without a Customs Broker. I consider myself lucky the way I could do it earlier, but now I would not recommend doing this yourself because filling out the US Government forms for canceling your US title, and exporting the car out of the US, and then filling out all the Mexican required forms to import the car is very complex, involving peculiar terminology, and 3-5 days for the two sides to check and approve the paperwork. If you contact a reliable Customs Broker before you get to the border, they generally have all the details and paperwork in order, ready for you to sign, and complete the process in just 3 – 5 hours versus 3-5 days for doing it yourself. The costs vary widely between crossing points and brokers, from low costs at Mexicali and Nogales, ranging up to 2x to 4x higher at Texas border crossings.

Tourist visa or becoming a Permanent Resident

That FMT (see earlier) is called a tourist card for a reason. If you become a home owner this card is not the right thing for you.
Since November 2012, gringos all over Baja with temporary tourist visa have been struggling to get their FM2 or 3's replaced with the new Permanent Resident cards.

Things smoothed out a few years later, but the following is an account of what a struggle it can be to obtain this much sought after, convenience card. Before that November, the temporary tourist visa had to be renewed each year exactly within the same month as it was originally applied for. As the process took about 2 to 3 weeks, one had to be available those same weeks each year as earlier application was not possible and being late would result in expensive penalties. As the new card suggests permanent, it has no expiration date. he beauty is that you need no renewal and do not have to purchase the 24-dollar tourist card. It does not mean that the holder has the intention of living permanently in Mexico. Once you leave, you get an exit form to be kept in your passport until returning into Mexico.

As a homeowner in Mexico, one is not considered a tourist and in that case this card is required. It also makes things simpler while being in Mexico, as it allows you to open a bank account, acquire a seniors' discount card, have a Mexican driver's license, just to mention a few. How wonderful you might think: but read on, it really was a pain to obtain.

Once you have decided to live and stay longer in Mexico, changing your tourist status to a permanent status can be done, but is not easy as the following article that I wrote for "The Gringo Gazette" a few years back will tell you.

Visa Madness in La Paz

The morning we left for the immigration office in La Paz to follow-up on our visa application, it was quite a hoopla to get out of our Todos Santos neighborhood. Road repair made for a bumpy, jolting detour followed by more road construction at the north end of town, where the bypass was being made. Once we were cruising along Highway 19 in our dusty little Sidekick, we reached La Paz in just under an hour. Another detour right off the main drag into La Paz gave us the notion that this was going to be a day with more obstacles then we bargained for.

Arriving at the immigration office after picking up some cash from an ATM, we grabbed number 68 while 43 was at the counter. Whoa, 25 to go and the waiting room was already crowded. The last two chairs were occupied, one by bags from a man who was apparently picking up coffee for his wife, the other by a child who was playing cars. His mom put him on the floor, so I have a seat and I got my electronic reader out to finish 'Heart of Darkness' for as much as that was possible in all the chaos.

More people walked in and the guy with coffee also brought two McDonald's breakfasts that smelled up the place. They were obnoxious scents to some and tantalizing to others who eagerly looked for some French fries. An orderly came in to send both snacking breakfasters out. No food was allowed inside and after 25 minutes there was no progress with the call numbers. It was probably coffee break for the staff.

About five weeks earlier, we had dropped off our application for 'Residente Permanente' after 7 years because the annually renewable FM3 status was now unavailable. With the new system they have you check the Immigration website to see if you can come to the office for the next step. We hoped that would be for finger printing and then, after paying the stiff application fees, it would be off to Mexico City, the paperwork that is, and bingo, 3 weeks later we would have permanent resident status. No more mandatory annual trips to this stuffy immigration office in La Paz.

Suddenly a few call numbers moved along. Apparently, some people were done in a few minutes while others took half an hour. There were mostly older folks, retired for years, going through the same process. The younger ones were here for temporary visa or work permits. The cramped atmosphere made you almost feel like a criminal. Some people in the room looked like it, but I hoped they were not.

There were agents carrying stacks of applications. One of them we recognized as a lawyer we visited once here in La Paz. He would charge 250 dollars an hour for his service. Today he was obviously wasting someone else's money as he had to wait just as long as everyone else. During a free consultation with him, he spent most of the time talking about himself and telling us, that he liked to frequent the gay bars in Cabo. He said he loved to cross-dress and when I saw him here with the pile of papers on his knees, in a three-piece suit and looking over his gold-rimmed spectacles, trying to make notes while squeezed between two chubby ladies, I wondered how he would look in a Cabo bar on Saturday night.

Then suddenly, two numbers in a row were called, for which nobody shows. They must have left the madhouse in lieu of better things to do. But the girls behind the counter were not too quick to catch on, and they waited and waited before they called the next number. You can feel the aggravation building in the crowded waiting room.

An energetic lady in black spandex sitting next to me was sitting on the edge of her chair in start mode, ready to run to the counter as hers was the next number about to come up. When called, she screamed hooray, waved her papers above her head and was ecstatic that her turn finally came up. The orderly needed to come out again and settle things down a bit. Another couple with coffee had to finish it outside. More people came and went, and as a matter of fact, we met nearly half the population of our Todos Santos neighborhood out here.

After about an hour and a half it was our turn. A short native girl was looking for our files. When she found them and opened them up, two letters fell out, notifications for more requirements but she could not explain or translate what it was all about. The girl who took our application five weeks ago, obviously didn't check things right and it looks like there could be some serious delays. An older and familiar face came up to the counter: Roberto who has worked here for years. He explained in almost perfect English what our problem was.

Mexican immigration law is a work in progress with too many

loopholes for different interpretations. While we were in the process, they changed the requirements: they now need a six-month review of your financial situation. Luckily, I can produce all they ask for right on the spot, except for the money, which can only be paid at a bank anyway. So we drove to Office Depot for a few sets of copies of the financial statements and stopped by a bank to pay the exorbitant application fees. Back following the detour off the main drag again, we made it just before the office closed. With all obligations filled we expected to be finger-printed now, but that proves to be too optimistic.

"Someone independent has to go over those copies and payments you supplied," Roberto explained.

"No problema," he says, "you did what you could and to have this reviewed it will only take 24 hours or a bit longer" he told us. 'Longer', that is to be the key-word here.

"Friday or Monday you will see the message on the website to come back in," Roberto assured us.

A week later there is still nothing on the website. We are now almost two months in to the process, and what is really discouraging to hear from other gringos is that some have been waiting since November. What strikes me when thinking about the term 'permanent resident', is that it is an illusive term, a plain impossibility as nothing is permanent or forever. What seems to be 'permanent' to me is the waiting.

Another week later we decided to go back to La Paz to see the status on our application. Unexpectedly, everything seemed to be in order and we were ready for finger printing. Yes, all ten fingers; a very messy affair, but as we hoped to pick up our long awaited and highly desired 'permanent resident' card, you take it. After putting our signature down, everything can now go to Mexico City for approval and in about 10-12 business days the cards should be ready for pick-up.

A few weeks later, despite having heard some horror stories about cards going astray or having the wrong nationality on it, I was very relaxed driving up to the immigration office, convinced this would be our last trip for that purpose. No detours this morning, a smooth ride into town and we even pulled a low number this time. The wait was not as long as before, all good signs up to the point that the immigration employee found our files and tried to open our envelopes containing the desired cards from Mexico City. As there was not one letter opener in the entire office, the guy used a paper clip, unfolds it and tries to unzip the envelopes which took excruciatingly long time for two people who were so eager to see their resident cards. My wives came out first and looked great. Mine came next, but I don't recognize the picture. A closer look brought shock, surprise and anger as it had a picture of another person.

"Don't say a thing, just take it," my wife says.

I say, "Deary, imagine I need this thing for identification one day and then they find out it is not me? Then what? I can't do that."

But of course, I also realized that with telling the officer, who had not spotted the mistake, it would create a lot of problems for us since we were planning to go back north, to leave Mexico within a week.

Closer examination of the card shows my name and birth date right, another guy's picture and a lady's signature on the back. Judy someone, a total misfit and absolutely useless. You would think they would be apologetic in the office, but oh no.

"You wait right there, and we will find out what to do," the officer said. So, we were back to this long waiting process that I had hoped would have been history by now. I paid 4,800 pesos to never come back to La Paz in that stuffy immigration office for this appalling waiting ritual.

The officer returned and told me "If you want to leave the country you need a permit as long as your card is not ready."

I requested to see a supervisor and she told me that they will fast-track my request and that in a week or 10 days they might have my card back. "But we cannot guarantee that," she adds *with a face, "don't blame me." I explain that we cannot wait for that and that we have to depart this weekend.*

"You need that exit permit in that case,' she told me again.

"OK," I said, "as long as I don't have to pay for that permit." But they expected me to go to a bank, pay 350 pesos more and come back and wait in line again for that special exit permit. And that was not the only problem with it. That permit would only be good for 2 months and within that time period I would have to come back and pick up my new card. All this was totally unacceptable to me, so I asked to see the director and have a word with him.

"OK," she said, "but wait out there." And so we were back in the stuffy waiting room for another 45 minutes. Our entire morning was flying by and so was our mood to celebrate our permanent status with a fancy lunch in town. Now I was wondering, "is my whole file gone? Do they need new fingerprints and photos again? What do I have to do to make this right?" Not an easy task apparently, in such a dysfunctional office where there are no letter openers and one day, they could not take finger prints as the ink-pad was as dry as a week old crusty dinner roll. "Just come back another day and we'll do you then." No regard for where you came from, in or out of town, who cares. It's your problem not theirs.

When I was finally led to the director's office, he became somewhat apologetic and told us there was "no problema. Just a small mistake from the Mexico City office. We'll have your new card in a week or maybe two."

He let one of his secretaries' dig into the files and thank god, she came up with my file complete with pictures and fingerprints that were still good. They would send everything off to Mexico City again and it would be back in a week or 10 days, but that was outside of their control, so it could be longer.

Very disappointed, we returned to Todos Santos and stopped by a lawyer's office to inquire what it would cost for him to pick up my card when ready. It became clear, it was not the cost, but the paperwork, the authorization that I, myself, had to file in the La Paz office to get this in order. The next day, off to La Paz again. This time it was late morning and I was hoping I would make it in before the one o' clock closing time. City traffic was backed up by the large arroyo south of Sorianas and the lights were all against me, but despite that I made it in at 13 minutes to one. Only one booth was open and one person ahead of me. First thing the girl said to me when I handed her my papers, "this has to be done by your lawyer."

I say, "no no, I was told specifically to do this myself."

"Oh, this is a change in your file?"

"Yes, it has to be added because I am off to the mainland," I made up a small white lie, as leaving the country without papers is illegal, "so my lawyer can pick it up for me."

"OK," she says, looks it over a second time and says "OK, that's all." I asked her once more to make sure to put it in the right file as mistakes have been made before, that's why I am here for the ninth time. Five weeks later I got an e-mail from the lawyer that he had my card and put it by UPS to my address up north.

My advice to folks that still must go through this process; take a lawyer or agent right from the start if you want to avoid numerous trips to the office. For about $100 - $200 extra, it can save you a lot of aggravation

-0-0-0-0-

Insurance, Medical and Mexican Auto insurance if you drive in Mexico.

Most people purchase medical/travel insurance before they go to Mexico: not just for curing Montezuma's revenge but for a multitude of unfortunate things that can happen while traveling abroad. Mind you, medical attendance, minor or serious hospitalized situations are much less expensive than in the US or Canada. My bill for five days private care in a good hospital with surgery on Saturday night and several specialists taking care of my unfortunate accident came to just over 7,000 Canadian $ (no more than 5,000 US). Still when a procedure or condition requires you to be airlifted home, it would be nice to have good insurance in place.

Don't drive in Mexico without purchasing special Mexican auto insurance because you can be thrown in jail if you don't have it. Your U.S. or Canadian insurance policy is not recognized or valid in Mexico. The minimum you need is a liability-only Mexican auto insurance policy to fulfill the legal requirement in the case of an accident.

There are so many choices with so many options. Let's first talk about American or Canadian licensed cars, as insurance for Mexican licensed cars is quite different. US and Canadian car insurance companies do not insure for Mexico, so one has to buy Mexican car insurance which can be done in the US. I always purchased our Mexican Insurance on line before we left home and estimated our arrival date at the border for the start date. You can buy it also at the border, but why spend time going into offices near busy border crossings and argue to get the best deal, if you can plan it ahead and buy on line. Google 'car insurance Mexico' and a plethora of companies come up. Decide on the date you plan to enter Mexico and whereas rates are different for Baja California and Sonora State as opposed to the rest of Mexico. Some companies apply the lower Baja rate to more States like Sinaloa and even down to Nyarit and Jalisco. 'Discover Baja' at http://www.discoverbajaonline.com/ is one of many companies that will give you quotes on line.

You can fill in the details about make and year and get a quote on line before you decide. A premium for a year policy is not much more than for 6 months, so I always bought the yearlong insurance.

Now if you keep your paperwork, proof of entering Mexico and accommodation and fuel bills you can claim the portion of your Canadian or US insurance back as that they did not have to insure your car as you were out of their insured area. It requires some paperwork but pays off if it is for an extended stay, and avoids you paying twice for car insurance.

Getting Mexican plates on your car? First you need a Mexican Driver's License.

The year before I had my car imported, I never got around to finish the process of getting Mexican license plates on it until the next winter in Mexico. Now it was one of my priorities to get it done. Where does one start? First plates and then insurance, or the other way around?

I was assured by the insurance rep that you don't need plates to insure the car. OK, but can I drive it with a foreign driver's license? Yes, you can, *'no problema,'* he assured me. Next, I went to the municipal's police station to get the plates. As it happened, I parked right under the window of the traffic office with expired Canadian plates. I was convinced with all the paperwork and copies that I had with me, I would come out that office with Mexican plates, safe to drive off.

Even at an early hour, there were already three or four people ahead of me. The dusty little office, smaller than my dining room, had only three chairs, one ancient metal desk with an antique typewriter and a small desk in the corner with an old desktop computer that was out of order. There was standing room only and people were arguing as far as I could understand about traffic violations. Not a relaxed atmosphere to say the least. When my turn came up to get my license plates, it became clear that I missed a few crucial papers of which one was a Mexican driver's license.

"When can I take the test," I asked in broken Spanish.

They were just done the week before, so it would take another month, I understood. I also needed a certificate with my blood-type before I could take the test. For that I had to go to the lab next week. What do I do in the meantime? Do I just walk out of the office, go to my car which was in plain view of the officer and drive away? I decided to wait a few minutes so that he was occupied with the next victim. Then I sneaked into my car and pulled away. I called my insurance guy who had promised me it would be so simple. He got me, at a price, temporary plates so I could drive around without the anxiety of being flagged down any minute.

After my blood test the following week, I stopped by the police station to find out when exactly the next drivers tests were provided. Then the same guy from last week asked me if I had an FM2 or 3. I showed him my temporary one since the original was in La Paz for renewal. This temporal paper had *'turista'* on it which he objected to since it was not good enough for getting a driver's license. I went to my car and got an actual copy of my FM3 which had the right terminology on it; *Rentista*. That was good, but since this copy was the page with my picture, it had the original issue date of 2007 on it.

"Why not current?" he asked me.

"Is in La Paz for extension," I explained once more.

"OK, you also need proof of living here, a water or electric bill," he made clear.

I went back to my car again because I thought to have a bill between all my paperwork in the glove-compartment. When I came back there was still nobody else in his office, so I got all the attention. He started opening huge drawers from a large steel filing cabinet and put some papers on the desk and started to fill out my name on them and other data that he took from my papers. Before I noticed, he put a legal-size paper in front of me with 20 multiple choice questions about traffic signs. I could not believe my eyes. I was not prepared for this, but eh, this is progress. Let's go for it. At that moment my cell-phone rang. In respect to this officer for letting me take the test, I answered very briefly because I expected a call that I didn't wanted to miss.

The first three or four questions looked pretty easy, but then the confusion settled in. It was not necessarily the longest answer, a technique I applied all my life when in doubt with multiple choice tests. Yes, I am a fraud, I realized. But before I was done, the officer filled out my license papers and asked for how many years I wanted it.

He put a small carbon paper in the age-old typewriter and asks the spelling of my name again. He was typing the bill that I had to pay, a fee of 447.51 pesos, at the municipal treasurer's office next door. So, was that it? My picture that I brought was already stamped and attached to the forms and I got the sweet feeling that I had the license in my pocket. When I came back with my proof of payment he wrote a few lines on the back of my paper which was apparently my temporary license. 'Come back next month on the 19th at 10 am, there will be a camera here and the official picture taking. Congratulations!'

"What's my score?" I asked. No answer, he was already busy with someone else arguing about a traffic violation.

My advice for taking the test; know a bit of Spanish and use your imagination with the picture signs. A blue picture of a pyramid of some sort, is this Egypt? No, it is the sign of an archaeological site coming up near you. A blue sign with a fork and a knife and 500 m below it. What do you think that means? A Hospital with a cantina? 500 miles to the next restaurant or might it be 500 meters? Know your *'curvas,'* three questions on *'curva peligrosa'*. Know the parking signs and what is right and left, and you will make it.

Good luck.

Now remember, if you have a Mexican license, you cannot legally operate a US registered vehicle, whether it is registered to you or not. However, in practice I have personally not seen any problems with this. But this is Mexico and the only thing you can count on is the weather, everything else can change overnight.

The final chapter on my car. How to get Mexican Plates on that Imported car.

The morning I went for my Mexican plates I also went to see the dentist in town. My entire life I avoided dentists like the plague, but as it turns out, she is a sweetheart and I don't mind going back to her again. I was 15 minutes early at the *dentista's* clinic because she only took 10 patients per morning and the waiting area was filling up.

I brought a good book as there could be a lot of waiting involved. "Eleven minutes" by Paul Coelho which I can highly recommend. An easy read, even in a crowded waiting area with kids crawling over the floor and screaming or yelling at times. I got my tooth fixed and with a numb lower lip and a strange feeling tongue, I went with my documents for my license plates to a *papeleria* on the main street where a cute girl does the copying for you. Two of each document, 16 copies total, I thought I had enough. Proud as a peacock because I had my new Mexican driver's license to show, I went to the police station with my stack of papers.

The most important requirements for getting plates are your Mexican Driver's license and the '*Pedimento*,' a declaration of the value of the car and proof of importation. The other things required are; a *Factura:* proof that the car is yours.
A water or electricity bill in your name as proof of your Mexican address.
An FM2 or FM3 (at that time), and lots of pesos for the different payments to be made and last but not least, 2 *copias* of all the documents.
The *Pedimento* proves that the import tax is paid and is supposed to be a green form which I didn't know at the time. When I prepared for the license plates application six weeks ago, I showed Senor Gonzales a copy of what I had, and he said resolutely "No good. Needs the original, green one."
I never got a green one when the importation was done. I called the guy who did the importation for me.
   "OK Sir, that can take a while, but I will get you the green one," he assured me.
He never answered as to why I didn't receive it in the first place: that's too fastidious. It took me six weeks of phone calls and e-mails without any progress. Rules and taxes have changed drastically this year, and not for the better. Then yesterday, I showed my white *Pedimento* with a purplish stamp on it to my insurance agent and he says "That's fine. Sometimes they don't come in green."
Oh nice, always exceptions to the rules. What have I been waiting for all this time?
At the traffic office, Senor Gonzales looks over all my documents and tells me I must take the paper work first to the *Secretaria de*

Finanzas for the state of Baja California Sur. Easy to find in Todos Santos, just across the *Centro Cultural*. Here two men behind a counter take my pile of papers, and while they look a bit puzzled with my not so green *Pedimento*, they start, to my surprise, entering data in their computer system. Twenty minutes later a bill runs off the printer and my registration for the 10-year-old Suzuki comes to 193 pesos and I got a sexy little 2"x3" sticker that had to go to the interior upper right windshield.

The vehicle must then be inspected to see that the VIN number being registered matches the paperwork. They also check your Mexican license to be sure you don't have any outstanding infractions, wants or warrants. Once this is verified, you will pay for the license plates, which came out to $ 754 pesos. Not bad, after I paid already 6,500 pesos in 2007 for importation. No more luxury tax on this car since it is over 10 years old. By the way, if you have a truck you never have to pay luxury tax. Anyway, I get about half of my papers back and went to Senor Gonzales at the police station to continue the process for my plates.

Senor Gonzales proved not to be Speedy Gonzales, he started from the beginning again, looking over the papers, scrutinizing everything. Then he wanted to see the car. OK, it is parked not below his window this time, but close enough. He brought a pen and notepad and took the serial number down. Wow, they do take this seriously. He looked at the condition of the car. Popped his head inside, what for? Smelling for drugs? To look at the odometer perhaps. We went inside his office again., and he told me to get two copies of everything once again. There I went again, to the *papeleria*. The smile from the girl kept me sane.

Back at Senor Gonzales, he started making up a bill on his ancient typewriter. This was for the plates, the decals, the inspection, you name it. It adds up to 728.65 pesos to pay next door at the municipal office. In the lineup while noon was approaching, I could feel it in my stomach.

Back with the signed and stamped invoice, Senor Gonzales dived in his master drawer and came out with my plates, CZL-3779, sizzle with a C, and yet another form that he started to fill out. This one combined all my data with the new numbered plates. That form, once filled out, and the bill of payment have to be copied again, twice. The girl with the glorious smile must have been on break, now some grumpy old lady takes my money and does the copying. This is not helping my mood, but I am getting so close. How many more *copias* can it take?

Back at Senor Gonzales, he puts all the papers together in a file-folder which he puts on top of a huge pile of others that must have gone through the same hassles I did. Finally, I walked out of his little office with my plates in hand, smiling because I realized that those plates are for life, the car's life that is.

Three years later, renewing my driver's license

Living in a small town has its pros, but also its cons. That time I could not get my license renewed in town but had to go to the police station in La Paz, the state capital. I had been there many times before, not to pay speeding tickets or other fines, but to pay for the yearly registration stickers for the car. Sort of like a yearly road-tax. That station is a zoo at any time and particularly in the morning. But as it takes a considerable time, one must start the process early.

Don't forget your paperwork. Old license, proof of address by means of a water bill or electric bill. Your temporary visa or permanent residency card. Of course, they know your blood type now as it is on your license, but after 3 years, your health might have deteriorated, so a physical examination is now required. I had no idea about that but found someone who directed me to a Red Cross office where the physician on duty took me in the office and went through the process. Blood pressure, stethoscope on your chest, weight and length etc.

Eighty pesos later, I got a small piece of paper with the required signatures and stamps. Off to the Police station and back in line again. More forms to be taken to the cashier (another lineup) and then to the actual person who takes the picture and prints the new license. She asks you a lot of questions again to confirm you are the right guy to take the picture of.

You put your signature down on a small screen and after a lot of noise and rumbling from the computer, a brand-new license with picture and signature rolls out. Was I ready to leave the police station in a hurry! There are too many guys toting guns and pistols around there.

Money matters and does money matter?

The Mexican peso has gone from a relative strong position: 10 for a US dollar, down in value over a period of years to 17-18 for that same dollar. This has not affected house or rental prices much as they are all mostly offered in US currency.

However, anything that has to be imported has gone up drastically and is making life rather difficult for local, low and medium high-income earners in Mexico.

Just recently I paid 45 pesos for a nice Victoria bottle of beer at a restaurant while my wife's Perrier was 65, almost the price of a glass of wine. A cappuccino can cost now anywhere from 40-60 pesos. Despite the general rule that says, what goes up comes down, for some reason that does not apply to those prices. The time that a gringo could live comfortably on 500 dollars a month is history.

Still, gringos are lucky with their strong dollar as they basically got 50% more pesos for their money compared with a few years ago.

For that matter, bringing pesos into Mexico does not make much sense. If you buy them at your local bank, it is often at a pretty unfavorable exchange rate. Border towns in the US often have more attractive rates and now many places, including the Pemex gas stations, accept credit cards, and ATM's are widely available. Up till only a few years ago obtaining gasoline was a strictly cash affair and open to some well-known scams hurting the uneducated or naive gringo.

When you fly in, many a times the ATM's are out of order at the airports so if you need pesos instantly, you can exchange your currency for pesos at *Cambios*, those special exchange kiosks at airports, border crossings and tourist areas.

Beware that not all ATM's are the same. I would avoid using one if it is not located inside or attached to a common known bank. Unfortunately, some have quite a low maximum withdrawal like Bancomer. Banamex, I found, has a much higher limit while the service charge is basically the same. At the time we bought our Mexican casa there was only one bank in town and a year later they had the first and only ATM installed. As we arrived to take possession of our house on November 1, I needed some extra pesos and as we arrived after banking hours, I counted on the ATM. When opening the glass door, to my surprise, I encountered a completely vacant little cubicle. Broken wires were sticking out of the wall and the ATM was gone. I never found out if it was a robbery the night before or a Halloween prank.

To get my drift: expect the unexpected in Mexico. The only thing you can count on is the weather, at least here in Mexico's Baja California Sur it is usually always sunny.

My recommendation is thus not to use any ATM's located outside of banks. Units at bars or grocery stores are less reliable and charge you an even higher service charge than the banks. I use the one at my bank preferably during hours the bank is open, for the simple reason, if the machine eats my card, I can go in and try to get my card back. Imagine losing your only card. Perhaps a good idea to have more than one bank card with you, particularly if you are staying longer than just for a short vacation.

-0-0-0-0-

Different Kind of Properties

Many people that have vacationed in the popular beach destinations know all about 'Time Shares.' The sales people can be very pushy, and folks are often trapped into something they later regret. Also, a week or two is not going to cut it if you like to live or retire in Mexico.
So, Time Share is out.

One has to make first the distinction between Restricted Zone and Non-Restricted land in Mexico as any land or property in the Restricted Zone has some complications for foreigners. A 50 kilometre strip along the entire Mexican coastline, East and West, is a restricted area for reasons to keep control over who owns what. Land border areas have even a wider strip, 100 km. that require special arrangements. Those old laws were revised in 1973 to accommodate foreign buyers. A Bank-Trust system called *Fideicomiso* was established which is a smart form of a 'milk-cow' set up by the Mexican government to keep a finger in the pot of all property owned by foreigners in border areas. This trust is held by a Mexican bank which will hold the property for a maximum duration of 50 years. The ocean is being considered a border also, requiring all property in Baja to have a bank trust which costs about 500 USD per year to keep up. The good news is that most Mexican banks are as good and trustworthy as most US banks are nowadays. There is no difference in use of the property for foreign owners and the trust is also fully transferable. It is just a lot of extra paperwork and expense to set it up and the yearly retaining fee to maintain.

-0-0-0-0-

Ejido Property

To get a good understanding of this type of property, I will go in deeper. Ejido property or land is owned by a community. So you should understand immediately the consequences of acquiring this type of property. There is a complicated approval process involved.
Each individual owner in that community got his piece of land after the re-distribution process that followed the revolution in 1917, after the dust had settled.

Up to 1992 Ejido land could not be sold. The government has changed that, but it can still take years before Ejido lots can change ownership because of the community involvement and wait times so other community members could buy the property in question for the same price as it is offered to a prospective buyer outside the community. For that matter I advise to stay away from such acquisitions.

Any property that is offered for sale in Mexico should be thoroughly checked out for title of ownership. There are companies that specialize in that, and I recommend that you use them.

The catch with selling your Mexican property

An important aspect of the huge currency fluctuations between dollar and peso is the capital gains tax when a gringo sells his property. Listing prices and offers are all in US currency but when the final price and contract at the lawyers is made up, the price is converted to pesos at the time of transaction.
Now imagine you bought a casita for 100.000 US in 2004 at 10

pesos to the dollar, it means the contract reads 1,000,000 pesos.

Now you sell 12 years later at 150,000 US. The price in pesos suddenly becomes 2,550,000 pesos with 17 pesos to the dollar resulting in a profit or capital gain of 1,550,000 pesos which will be taxable at a rate of around 30-35% (things fluctuate almost year to year) Even if you could sell it at the same price you paid for it, you make a peso profit of 700,000 x 35% meaning a tax bite of 245,000 pesos or about $ 14,000 USD. This can hurt!

The example has not taken into account the purchase and sale expenses that can be deducted from the profit of course, but still, be warned. Now imagine the peso will get stronger, this currency problem would become much less of a problem. But who knows what will happen.

Shopping in Mexico

Go where the locals shop would certainly help your grocery budget. But are you willing to adopt your diet with corn and beans, foreign veggies, fruit and fish? Friends of us catch fish almost on a daily basis and have a freezer full with more than they can handle. Depending on season, you can indulge in things that are expensive in the North, like avocados and mangoes. But items that are less common like gourmet and low-fat items like pancetta, Belgian endive or truffles, will be expensive. Anything imported will be expensive, so watch out. Eating out can be quite affordable depending on style of restaurant and if you drink wine or not.

From International Living Magazine I quote the following: *The key to smart shopping in Mexico is local shopping. You'll pay about 50 cents a kilo (that's about 2.2 pounds) for fresh fruit like mangoes, oranges, or pears. A kilo of avocados sells for about*

$1.55–which is roughly what you'd pay for one avocado in the U.S. While it is true that you can find just about any product you're used to having up north, it's also true that you'll probably pay more for the convenience of a brand name. But if you shop at the local produce markets and the stores where locals buy, you're sure to pay less for your goods.

For more accurate information, there is a 'Cost of living in Mexico' web-link https://is.gd/2HdSPr
It claims that as of May 2016, the cost of living in Mexico is 58% lower than in the US and 51.47% lower than in Canada (aggregate data for all cities, rent is not taken into account).

Gasoline and Diesel in Mexico

Another important part of your expense in Mexico is gas, if you drive a lot. Gas stations up until the time of writing are run by the state-owned company called Pemex and gasoline was about $ 3.25/gallon. There is talk about US companies opening up shop: Gulf being one of them, starting with 4 stations in 2016 expanding to 500 stations the following year. Up to the time of writing, the price was fixed all over the country and was very reasonable up to a few years ago. But now, the price of gasoline equals, or is even higher than the one in the US state of California. I don't understand how Mexicans with an average hourly wage of around 2 dollars (depending on skill) can pay for gasoline to drive a car. (Average daily wage was 290 pesos in early 2016. as reported by the Secretariat of Labour & Social Welfare, Mexico.) I paid 600 pesos for a full tank the other day. It might last me a week or two as I don't drive much, or rather use my bicycle or walk to stores.
Diesel is higher in price then gasoline and most of Mexico does not have the Ultra-Low Sulfur as is required for most newer diesel

(after 2007-8) models. The cut-off for models is around 2007. Any car newer, requires the 'Ultra Low Sulfur' which is OK at gas stations in Baja California Norte and other areas close to the American border.

Now don't be surprised when you have a car with a fuel tank capacity of 60 liters, that they can pump 66 liters in your tank when it was almost empty. Despite so called regular calibrations of the gas-pumps, individual franchise owners like to make an extra buck here and there. This seems to happen particularly in touristy areas. And gringo beware, as if this is not enough of a rip-off, the pump attendants have their own smart tricks in shortchanging you with your unfamiliar peso notes. Some attendants have magician's hand tricks showing you a 50-peso bill that you supposedly gave them instead of a 500 bill. Anyway, all this might change for the better when foreign oil companies will move in to open up some competition which is something unheard of until now in Mexico. In the telecom business this monopoly still has to be broken up as Mr. Carlos Slim, interchangeably with Bill Gates, is not without cause, the richest man on earth.

Utilities

Electricity

Like Pemex for gasoline, there is only one national electric company called CFE (Comisión Federal de Electricidad). Since we were connected a few years ago (were on solar before) I have been quite impressed with their service considering they have no competition other than from the sun. Solar-powered homes in Baja are quite common. But as for CFE, we have lost power a number of times.

Once it was for an extended period of time, as it was after hurricane Odile. But generally, service is back up in an hour or two. In winter, when not using air-conditioning, the 2-month bill was very little as our use stayed below 1200 kwh per month.

There is a break-point at 1200 kwh/month where the price goes up remarkably and another at 2500 kwh/month. At this latter point, you will be paying around double what you might pay in most US cities. Things that will impact your bill are pool pumps, air-conditioners and electrical heaters. CFE is not very forgivable in terms of late pay. They cut you off rather quickly. To avoid that you can set up an automatic payment with your Mexican bank or pay on line.

Propane

Most homes use propane for water heaters and cooking stoves. We used to have our fridge on propane, something I would not recommend if you can have an electric one. We had the large tank that only needed to be refilled every three or four months like most newer homes have. But you can also have the slender green bottles that are supplied by a different company.

Trucks will come by once or twice a week, honking loudly or playing a tune over a loudspeaker. A fill for a larger tank is now quite expensive as it can run close to some 1000 pesos. If you use it only for hot water and cooking, this will last you a long time.

Satellite TV, telephone and internet

The days of going to an internet cafe are long over, at least in our neck of the desert and if you can afford 50 dollars US for Wi-Fi. Lots of places such as coffee shops and restaurants offer free Wi-Fi now, and people that do not have their private connection are happy to go there on a regular basis. OK if you are here for a short time, but living full-time or retiring here might warrant a better solution. If you live or rent in a neighborhood that has a land-line for telephone from Tel Mex, Mr. Slim can connect you with his DSL service to the internet. This monthly bill can be set up as an auto-payment with your Mexican bank. And there are 'stickies' you can use and take your laptop anywhere you want.

We had no land-line, so a cellphone was the solution and there are many different plans available for that.

Cable has become available in some neighborhoods while streaming shows over the Internet is becoming the norm. Most people however, watch TV received by satellite. Dish-TV is apparently the most popular, but we hated it as it was on East-coast time. And it was expensive at around $ 100. US a month.

On obtaining a cellphone, Chuck Poulson, travel writer and blogger, wrote the following rather surprising method used in Mexico in the spirit of trying to do something about trafficking and what not. According to him, it isn't helping much, but boy, are they trying.

"I joined the 21st century," Chuck explains, "and bought a smart phone. To get a plan for the phone through the near-monopoly TelMex, I had to provide the following:
1. Proof that I'm residing here, a bureaucratic ordeal unto itself
2. Passport.
3. Three local references. I paid with VISA for the phone and plan, so it wasn't a matter of credit worthiness
4. A visit at my residence by "authorities" to make sure I wasn't a cyberspace robot or had a meth lab in the kitchen".

Last but not least: water

Infrastructure in general has improved substantially since we arrived for long-term stays in 2004. This does not mean that you will have reliable water pressure day and night. It all depends on where you are and I would make serious inquiries about water supply before you put any money down for a property.

Be sure you understand the source and fees for the water you are going to need. Interrupted service or pressure can be accommodated with large tanks on rooftops as you might have seen in many places. If interruptions become more then occasionally, a large in-ground cistern might be required. We have been expanding our water reserve over the years on an ongoing basis, as town's service became less reliable over time. We also had access to Ejido water. A lovely canal would run simply water on command. Then it became twice a week, once a week and nothing for weeks during dry periods. The garden suffered mostly from that as that water, of course, was not suitable for in house. Still, to this date we buy the large blue bottles (19 liters) of water for drinking, tea and coffee and washing veggies. An in-house filter system could avoid bringing the heavy bottles home two or three times a week.

Having said all this, we feel still fortunate not to have the water truck to fill us up every so often. For certain areas there is no choice and it is normal to have water trucked in at about 85 or 90 dollars once a month. Compare that with our monthly water bill of around 100 pesos (around 6 dollars US), you realize it makes sense to find out what your situation is going to be like.

For Shade, Palm trees come in handy

Now assuming you found your idyllic place, keep in mind that in a sunny country, shade is important. This is 101 on palm trees. The first thing Mexican do when they buy land to build on is planting palm trees because it takes time to grow.

Ever heard of a Jelly Palm? The other day I was browsing at a nursery for some high scrubs as I needed to create some shade and privacy between my place and the neighbors. As it was basically to protect me from the view they have from their second-floor guest casita, located above their garage, the tree I was looking for should be at about 12'-18' tall.

At that height, palms come to mind, but it can take a long time before they will grow to that level. Even ordinary Washingtonians, the poor-man's palm, can take 5 or 6 years before they reach my required height. And the problem then is that they keep growing, as they can reach 80-90 feet and become bare at 18 or 20 feet level. For that reason, I went looking for other species and got myself informed on the much prettier Royal palm. Scientific name is Roystonea and Wikipedia tells me that the 'royal' is just one of eleven species of monoecius palms, native to the Caribbean Islands, and the adjacent coasts of Florida and Central and South America.

An interesting fact is that this genus was named for Roy Stone, a US army engineer. But as the royal palm can reach heights of 130 ft, this one is not going to do the trick for me either. Most species in this group will grow between the 49'-66' range. It will take longer for what is left of my life-time to see the appropriate height.

Of course, there is a solution for that: transplant some more mature palms, but that becomes quite oppressive for my peso account. You do see it more and more: whole palms including a massive clod of soil and roots transported through town. I went to see someone at a *Vivero*, as they call a nursery here, to find out what they recommend. The guy told me: Jelly' palms. What? Are you kidding? I have heard of jelly beans but never of jelly palms. The arborist told me that Butia Capitata, the official name for a Jelly Palm, is one of the hardiest feather palms, tolerating temperatures below freezing and is commonly grown on the East Coast of the United States as far north as Virginia Beach, Virginia and West up to Seattle, Washington. We joked about climate change and how I wished we didn't need such a hardy palm here in Baja. I explained my need to obscure the neighbors casita at a certain height. And then he was right on the ball when he told me that this palm grew up to 18-20 ft., exactly what I needed. He showed me some mature Jelly palms as we walked over the grounds to the back of his *vivero.*

At home I looked up some more on the Jelly palm and found out that it carried edible fruit. Ripe Jelly palm fruit is about the size of large cherries, and yellowish/orange in color. The taste is a mixture of pineapple, apricot, and vanilla according to Wikipedia. The taste can vary depending on soil conditions, perhaps some banana taste can be detected. It is tart and sweet at the same time, with flesh like a loquat (Chinese plum), but slightly more fibrous. The last fact is an absolute bonus if you realize that the pulp is a good source of Beta Carotene and pro-vitamin A according to Juliana Pereira Faria, PhD who published her findings in an abstract.

Years ago, the mansion at the end of our road got four truckloads, those long 16-wheeler, with mature palms delivered and planted. Then they found out they were not the Royals but the rather poor looking Mexican Washingtonians.
Not good enough of course for a mansion, so a few weeks later

they were pulled out and new truckloads arrived late at night to put the right ones in. Money was obviously no object. I am in a different category, but the more I found out about the Jelly palm, the stronger I was motivated to order a few mature ones and just hope they will catch on as I will invest most of my peso account to regain my privacy, and more importantly; shade, and perhaps have some healthy fruit along the way.

-0-0-0-0-

Conclusion

Mexico has been for me an adventure, a wonderful daily tonic when I am there and a place for exciting personal growth. This can be of course, the same for you. Your decision to live or retire here may be based on emotion, but make sure that you substantiate it with sound information, common sense and above all, reflection from whatever it is that moves you.

-0-0-0-0-

Glossary

Aduanas, customs
ahora, now
bocana, estuary
Bomberos, firefighters
calle, street
callejonadas, street parades
cambio, change, ex-change booth
Camino, road
cantina, bar or cafetaria
casita, small house or cottage,
cavalcade, horse parade
cerveza, beer
cerveza clara, Lager beer
cerveza negra, dark beer
chihuahua, Small dog-breed, name of State in Mexico and city
chubasco, summer rain storm
copia, copy
Cucaracha, cockroache
curva, turn (in a road)
dentista, dentist
denuncia, official crime report
Equipal, handcrafted furniture
factura, invoice, or bill
Federales, State police
Fideicomiso, fides (trust) and committere (to commit),
    meaning that something is committed to one's trust. In
    this case a bank holds title of Mexican property in trust
    for foreign owners.
Fiesta, party, public holiday
Finiquito, severance package
Fronterra, border
gringo, gringa, American man, woman
hasta luego, Talk to you later
Hojas Pedimento, import/export papers
Isla, island
jalapeño, hot pepper

La Vida Loca, the crazy life-style
Malecón, boulevard, road along waterfront
mañana, tomorrow
Martes, Tuesday
mas o menos, more or less
Ministerio Publico, Public Ministry
milagro, miracle
mordida, the bite, pay-off
negra, dark
norte, north
palapa, open-sided dwelling with a <u>thatched</u> roof made of dried <u>palm</u> leaves
panga, fishing boat
papel, paper, piece of paper
papeleria, stationary store
peligrosa, dangerous
pescadero, fisherman
pescado, fish
permanente, permanent
Peublo, village
playa, beach
problema, problem
Santos, saint
sarape or serape is a long blanket-like shawl
Semana Santa, Holy week, the week before Easter
sopa, soup
rentista, retired
Residente, resident
transito, transit
todos, all-inclusive
turista, touris
vivero, nursery for plants
zocalo, center of town, main square

Acknowledgements

First, I'd like to thank my wife of nearly 50 years, Marianne who traveled with me most of the time and with whom I shared these many experiences. Most were pleasant, some were not so pleasant, while living in Mexico. She played an integral role in our lives in Mexico and encouraged me to write this book and made my sometimes steep learning curve, manageable.

To my friends and family, let me express my gratitude in helping me to decide on the right cover and other ideas. And last but not least, the content was tirelessly proofread and edited by Wendy Tippett, Tony Hargreaves and Stuart Swain. Without those three, this book wouldn't be readable.

This book is the follow-up on 'A Taste in Mexico,' which is still available as an e-book and in print. Both books are my own creation and I apologize for any imperfections, changed conditions or facts as Mexico is a very dynamic country where change can happen rather rapidly.

-0-0-0-0-

51888729R00098

Made in the USA
Lexington, KY
07 September 2019